Such was prize-fighting's appeal during
that, at its zenith, the sport was patronised by royalty and aristocracy and, notwithstanding its illegality, its contests often attracted thousands of spectators from all walks of life. *Up to Scratch* covers bareknuckle fighting from early English stage bouts to boxing's transitional period between knuckles and gloves.

Although concentrating mainly on a region, then just north of the metropolis, which was a favourite venue of the London prize-ring, it is essentially an anecdotal account of what was unquestionably one of England's most dramatic sporting pastimes. Included are tales of some of the great champions – Tom Johnson, Daniel Mendoza, Jem Belcher, Tom Sayers and Jem Mace – as well as many forgotten, but no less colourful, fistic heroes.

Up to Scratch powerfully evokes an age when pugilism was a barbaric, corrupt and yet primarily noble activity which makes today's boxing look positively tame by comparison.

During five years of extensive research through contemporary newspapers, the author located much previously unpublished material appertaining to the prize-ring and the many fascinating characters of the sport.

An experienced kick boxer and martial artist, Tony Gee's avid interest in boxing stems from a very early age and his fascination with prize-fighting has led to years of extensive research.

He is a contributor on this subject to the *New Dictionary of National Biography* and is now considered one of the country's leading historians of the prize-ring. His next published work will be on the history of the prize-ring in Scotland which he is currently researching.

Tony Gee was born in Finchley, North London, and now lives nearby in Potters Bar.

UP TO SCRATCH

**Bareknuckle Fighting
and Heroes of the Prize-ring**

TONY GEE

Queen Anne Press

First published in 1998 by
Queen Anne Press
a division of
Lennard Associates Ltd
Mackerye End, Harpenden
Herts AL5 5DR

First paperback edition published in 2001

A catalogue entry is available from the British Library.

ISBN 1 85291 642 7

Production Editor: Ian Osborn
Jacket design: Design 2 Print

Printed and bound in Great Britain by
Selwood Printing Ltd. West Sussex

CONTENTS

LIST OF ILLUSTRATIONS

FOREWORD

I have always been interested in the era of bareknuckle fighting. It was a brutal sport in those far-off days but, without a doubt, it also contained a certain nobility. I am reminded of this whenever I look at the old boxing pictures hanging on my wall and likewise when I read *Up to Scratch*. The author has obviously been extremely thorough in his research and has done an excellent job of finding out about the many mills and dramas that took place in a very popular, but now forgotten, pugilistic venue. I was fascinated to read that such a large slice of boxing history actually happened in an area which I know well, and which is not far from my former home.

What amazes me most about the fighters in this period was their remarkable endurance. Imagine having to fight 127 rounds, lasting 147 minutes, like Ned Savage and Jem Wallace did at Whetstone. A far cry from the maximum 12-round contests of today – no wonder both men were carried off insensible at the end. It also surprises me how many spectators consistently attended prize-fights bearing in mind the dangers they faced and the long distances they often had to walk. Would any of today's boxing fans put themselves out to such an extent?

This book is a very welcome addition to the ranks of prize-fighting literature. It will be equally well received by both serious students of the early days of boxing and those who just enjoy reading about the sport.

SIR HENRY COOPER
OBE, KSG

ACKNOWLEDGMENTS

I would like to thank the following individuals and institutions for their assistance in the writing of this book:

Mr Bill Matthews, prize-ring historian, for all his unstinting help and encouragement and for checking the manuscript.

Dr Pamela Taylor, archivist, of Barnet Local Studies and Archives, for checking the manuscript and providing information, advice and invaluable support.

Mrs Gillian Gear and Mrs Doreen Willcocks of Barnet and District Local History Society, Barnet Museum, and Mr Graham Javes, local historian, for making their knowledge of the area available to me.

Mr Brian Warren, archivist, Potters Bar and District History Society, for his kind help in supplying and verifying details on Kitts End.

Mr Harold Alderman, boxing historian, and Mrs Doreen Berger and Mr Raymond Foster, genealogists, for providing relevant material.

Mrs Daisy Durrant for supplying information on her grandfather, William Springall.

The staffs of the British Library and the British Library Newspaper Library, especially Mr Stewart Gillies.

The staff of Hertfordshire Record Office.

The staff of the Hertfordshire Local Studies Collection, Hertfordshire Libraries.

The staff of Hertfordshire Central Resources Library, Hatfield.

The staff of Chipping Barnet Library.

The staff of Church End Finchley Reference Library.

The staff of Cranborne Library, Potters Bar.

The staffs of Cemetery Management Limited, Islington Cemetery and St Pancras Cemetery for consulting records appertaining to St Marylebone, Islington and St Pancras Cemeteries, East Finchley.

Finally, I would like to express my very grateful thanks to my parents, Hazel and Leonard, for their assistance with research for this enterprise, as well as their unfailing support.

INTRODUCTION

A noble pastime, void of vain pretence –
The fine old English art of self-defence

Renton Nicholson

The Battle of Barnet (1471), one of the bloodiest conflicts of the Wars of the Roses, has been well documented, but little has been written about the many pugilistic battles to which Barnet and its surroundings have played host. In the following pages I aim to rectify such an oversight by giving the reader a glimpse into the part which this well-known area, then just north of the metropolis of London, played in the fascinating history of the 18th- and 19th-century English prize-ring. Most of the recorded skirmishes took place on Barnet Common, in fields surrounding the village of Whetstone or on the infamous Finchley Common, a favourite haunt of many a highwayman and footpad during the early bareknuckle era of boxing. (Dick Turpin was reputed to have hidden behind 'Turpin's Oak' at the London end of the common to lay in wait for victims, whilst Jack Sheppard, a thief famed for his amazing gaol breaks, was recaptured there following an audacious escape from Newgate Prison.)

Throughout its history, London was both the centre and proving ground for the sport. Although prize-ring activity in various provincial regions was particularly prevalent at times, in order for a fighter to establish a national reputation it was usually necessary for him to contend in metropolitan circles. The attraction of the Barnet area as a pugilistic venue for the London prize-ring lay primarily in its proximity to the capital and its county boundary position. Regarding the former, it was considered well within walking distance for the hardy fistic enthusiasts and, being on a main arterial road out of London, there were plenty of opportunities for them to quench their thirst along the route. The boundary position was significant inasmuch as it enabled a contest to be moved from Middlesex to Hertfordshire or vice versa should a magistrate in either of the counties decide to enforce the law. Consequently many of the most renowned bruisers of the day visited the locality, not just as participants but also in other related circumstances, together with more obscure but no less interesting characters. Of course, the district's important pugilistic role did not always find favour with the local populace, who were forced to endure the unruly mob behaviour which often accompanied a prize-fight. The landlords of its various public houses, however, certainly benefited, for fight followers were not normally noted for their sobriety.

Although mainly the story of the Barnet area's prize-ring links, the sport's many aspects are reflected fully – the saints and sinners (invariably more of the latter), the triumphs and tragedies, and especially the continual struggle against the forces of law and order, were all a constant feature nationwide. The approach taken has been a chronological anecdotal one and the account covers bareknuckle fighting from early English stage bouts, through an aristocratically backed heyday, to its gradual demise.

Occasional reference to fist-fighting in England can be found earlier than the 18th century but it is with James Figg that the story of modern pugilism really begins. Figg is generally considered to be the sport's first champion although, at the time, he was far more famous for his expertise with the sword and quarterstaff. Indeed it was usual for his many contests to be billed as trials of skill (featuring such weapons), rather than trials of manhood (involving fists). The Marquis de Bretagne, over a decade afterwards, recalled seeing a "certain Prize fighter called Figg, who handles a broad Sword with the greatest Dexterity of any Man alive". Not commonly known is that Figg was originally one of the scholars of the noted Timothy Buck of Clare Market, as can be seen by an advertisement in the *Daily Courant* (London's first daily newspaper) of 8 June 1714. A further notice in the same journal, in the autumn of that year, alerts us to the fact that, by then, Figg had certainly attained the position of "Master of the Noble Science of Defence". He later opened an amphitheatre where gentlemen about town could acquire knowledge of the manly arts and witness the top fighters of the day demonstrate their talents. There is no doubt that his establishment was a showcase for some of the best early exponents of regular boxing and, as such, a strong case can be made for considering him England's first pugilistic promoter. William Hogarth, the famous painter and engraver, depicted Figg in several of his works and also painted 'The March to Finchley', in the background of which is shown one of the earliest representations of a bareknuckle mill.

Whilst Figg could be said to have brought the sport into prominence initially, it is Jack Broughton who is generally credited with being its true founder. Originally a waterman and the 1730 winner of Doggett's Coat and Badge, one of the world's oldest sculling races, he laid down the prize-ring's first set of organized rules in 1743 for the better regulation of his own amphitheatre. These formed a framework for fair play and remained virtually unaltered for nearly 100 years until they were superseded following the tragic death of

RULES

TO BE OBSERVED IN ALL BATTLES ON THE STAGE

I. THAT a fquare of a Yard be chalked in the middle of the Stage; and on every frefh fet-to after a fall, or being parted from the rails, each Second is to bring his Man to the fide of the fquare, and place him oppofite to the other, and till they are fairly fet-to at the Lines, it fhall not be lawful for one to ftrike at the other.

II That, in order to prevent any Difputes, the time a Man lies after a fall, if the Second does not bring his Man to the fide of the fquare, within the fpace of half a minute, he fhall be deemed a beaten Man.

III. That in every main Battle, no perfon whatever fhall be upon the Stage, except the Principals and their Seconds; the fame rule to be obferved in bye-battles, except that in the latter, Mr. Broughton is allowed to be upon the Stage to keep decorum, and to affift Gentlemen in getting to their places, provided always he does not interfere in the Battle; and whoever pretends to infringe thefe Rules to be turned immediately out of the houfe. Every body is to quit the Stage as foon as the Champions are ftripped, before the fet-to.

IV. That no Champion be deemed beaten, unlefs he fails coming up to the line in the limited time, or that his own Second declares him beaten. No Second is to be allowed to afk his man's Adverfary any queftions, or advife him to give out.

V. That in bye-battles, the winning man to have two-thirds of the Money given, which fhall be publicly divided upon the Stage, notwithftanding any private agreements to the contrary.

VI. That to prevent Difputes, in every main Battle the Principals fhall, on coming on the Stage, choofe from among the gentlemen prefent two Umpires, who fhall abfolutely decide all Difputes that may arife about the Battle; and if the two Umpires cannot agree, the faid Umpires to choofe a third, who is to determine it.

VII. That no perfon is to hit his Adverfary when he is down, or feize him by the ham, the breeches, or any part below the waift: a man on his knees to be reckoned down.

1. Broughton's Rules (1743), which laid down the first code of practice for the prize-ring.

William Phelps after his contest with Owen Swift in March 1838. Broughton was also responsible for introducing gloves, then called 'mufflers', for sparring purposes, in order to protect his pupils "from the Inconveniency of black Eyes, broken Jaws and bloody Noses".

Unlike boxing today, under both Broughton's Rules and the later 'New Rules' of 1838, a round terminated when one of the protagonists was either punched, thrown or wrestled to the ground. Originally, a yard square was marked out in the middle of the ring, and the fighter's second had half a minute to bring his man to the line on their side of the square or he was declared the loser. The action of getting to this line was called 'coming up to the "mark" or "scratch" '. The regulation was amended slightly in the 'New Rules' so that at the end of half a minute, or a time previously agreed upon, a pugilist had eight seconds to reach, unaided, a mark in the centre of the ring or he was considered beaten.

Unfortunately, material on prize-fighting is somewhat sketchy for the sport's first few decades. To begin with, during the Figg and Broughton eras, newspapers printed advertisements for regular stage fights, but reports on these were few and far between. Later, as pugilism became subject to legal interference, the press in the main began to side with the authorities against what they perceived to be a barbaric pastime. The vast majority of bouts therefore went unrecorded. It was not until the revival in the fortunes of boxing towards the latter part of the 1780s, partly due to the influence of the future King George IV, that the fashionable papers of the day started to show increasing interest. Even *The Times*, which was vehemently against all fistic endeavours, felt obliged to include occasional items. In 1792 the *Sporting Magazine* arrived on the scene, and this monthly periodical did report milling in some detail. Nevertheless it took the appearance in 1822 of *Bell's Life in London and Sporting Chronicle* for truly extensive coverage of the prize-ring to feature regularly in a newspaper. (Before leaving the subject of newspaper reporting, it should be noted that the areas of East End, North End and Church End were then usually referred to merely as Finchley, and the same policy has likewise been adhered to throughout this book. However, most of the mentions of Finchley relate to East End, which is now known as East Finchley. All journals consulted for information are listed in a comprehensive bibliography at the end, together with books and other sources referred to.)

The earliest books to cover ring activities in any depth were *Pancratia, or a History of Pugilism*, attributed to William Oxberry, and Pierce Egan's *Boxiana; or, Sketches of [Ancient and] Modern Pugilism*. *Pancratia* was published in 1812, and the title page of the first volume of *Boxiana* also bore the same date. Oxberry was a versatile character who, in a relatively short life, engaged in the multiple occupations of writer, printer, actor and publican. Egan, a respected sporting journalist and one of the most popular writers of his age, was the foremost chronicler of the prize-ring and *Boxiana* is usually recognized as the definitive work on the subject. Nevertheless, it is not entirely exempt from errors and bias, since Egan had a marked propensity for exaggeration, particularly with regard to fighters of Irish origin.

Other journalists and authors of works on the bareknuckle era worthy of a mention include Jon Bee (real name John Badcock); Henry Downes Miles of *Pugilistica: The History of British Boxing* fame; father and son Vincent and Francis Dowling, editors of *Bell's Life* and compilers of the series of record books *Fistiana; or The Oracle of the Ring*; and Fred Henning, who wrote, albeit rather imaginatively, for the *Licensed Victuallers' Gazette* under the nom-de-plume of 'Tourist'. In addition, some acknowledgment should be made to George Kent, the bohemian and eccentric reporter for the *Weekly Dispatch* and the *British Luminary or Weekly Intelligencer*. His own newspaper, *Kent's Weekly Dispatch and Sporting Mercury*, was held in high esteem during its brief existence but, according to Egan, he failed to complete three or four boxing publications that he commenced. To all the above scribes and many lesser lights I owe my grateful thanks: without them the following could not have been written.

Tony Gee
London, September 1998

PART I - THE EARLY DAYS

Since boxing is a manly game,
And Britons' recreation,
By boxing we will raise our fame,
'Bove any other nation.

Anon

A Gypsy Prince

Finchley Common, at the height of the highwayman's domination, was host to a gypsy encampment which apparently brought forth one of the more intriguing characters of 18th-century pugilism. Pugnus, in his *History of the Prize Ring*, recounted how a gypsy prince by the name of Boswell decided on abdication whilst at Finchley in the spring of 1738 (although this date, as will be seen, is obviously incorrect). Both *Pancratia* and Pugnus thought Boswell to be the son of the king of the English Romanies, but others believed he was merely the nephew of the ruler of the Yorkshire clan. Whatever his exact claims as heir apparent, the gypsy community must have been extremely disconcerted when he renounced his exalted position in order to make his way as an independent adventurer in the metropolis.

Bareknuckle fighting has always traditionally been a favourite Romany pastime, and Benjamin Boswell had shown early fistic promise. It was not surprising, therefore, following a short period when he appears to have concentrated on the nefarious calling of highwayman, that he should resolve to try his hand as a professional pugilist. Boswell soon became a regular performer at the popular sporting venue the "Great Booth at Tottenham-Court" although, according to Pugnus, he used his fighting activities "as a blind for his more disreputable pursuits". He was obviously very busy since he also supplemented his earnings by working as a brickmaker (appropriately whilst living in Brick Street, Hyde Park Corner) and later embraced an occupation well suited to his strength, that of a chairman.

Details of Boswell's milling qualifications can be found in Captain John Godfrey's *A Treatise upon the Useful Science of Defence*. Written when the pugilist was still active, Godfrey described that, amongst other attributes, he possessed "a particular Blow with his left Hand at the Jaw, which comes almost as hard as a little Horse kicks". However, it was the Captain's opinion that he lacked the one requisite essential to be a complete boxer, namely "true English Bottom". There is no evidence to support this assertion in the journals of the day, but the author's view has to be respected as the esteemed Godfrey had been an accomplished amateur sportsman and a diligent pupil of James Figg.

Since Boswell was known to have fought often on the stage at the Great Booth, it is somewhat odd to find that only a single set-to is usually attributed to him by ring historians. This was a losing fight on 16 June 1741 against George Taylor, who was second only to Jack Broughton as the best boxer of the post-Figg age. The oversight cannot be accounted for by the explanation that Boswell's other bouts were not chronicled at the time as, for instance, an earlier fight with Taylor was publicized and reported in the *Daily Advertiser* in October 1739. On 6 October the newspaper emphasized the large amounts of money that were depending on the ensuing battle whilst a notice one week later advised that the match itself was for £100 and offered tickets for the stage at three shillings each. The contest took place at Tottenham-Court on 16 October and Taylor suffered what was undoubtedly an unexpected defeat "after a stout Engagement, which lasted sixteen Minutes".

In line with the general trend for a boxer of the era to have regular fights with the same adversary, it is highly probable that Boswell and Taylor faced each other on at least five other occasions. They were certainly billed to meet on 6 December 1737, while an advertisement for a clash between the two, scheduled for 11 January 1740, intimated that their previous "long and doubtful" affair had occurred at the end of 1739. In addition, notices appeared in the *Daily Advertiser* in March of both 1741 and 1743 detailing further proposed confrontations between these perennial protagonists.

At this point it is worth noting the possibility that Taylor himself visited Barnet. Originally a barber and peruke maker, he became proprietor of the Great Booth but later relinquished it following the success of Broughton's Amphitheatre. After a spell exhibiting at his rival's establishment, he was mentioned, in January 1750, as having lately been dismissed as a "Keeper of Enfield-Chace" (which bordered on the Barnet area) under "such Circumstances as when made known he doubts not will recommend him to the Compassion of the Publick [sic]". By July of the same year he was well established as landlord of the Fountain at Deptford, a situation which he stated he was enabled to enter into because of public generosity.

Another celebrated performer against whom Boswell definitely contended was James Field the Sailor. Their fight, which was described as "one of the sharpest that has been for a considerable time", occurred on 15 November 1743. Victory for the underdog,

Field, earned him a chance to oppose Taylor some three weeks later. Although defeated on that occasion, Field afterwards showed his ability by extending Broughton's future conqueror, Jack Slack, in a desperate battle lasting 1 hour and 32 minutes. Even more than Boswell, Field has inexplicably been ignored by historians. Like the gypsy pugilist, he also had criminal propensities and his fistic career was brought to an abrupt end when he was executed at Tyburn on 11 February 1751. Interestingly, his skeleton is featured in 'The Four Stages of Cruelty', Hogarth's final series of pictorial morality sermons illustrating the wages of sin.

Further notices in the *Daily Advertiser* promoting other planned Boswell appearances included an early one in November 1737 with John Read, commonly known as 'Hammersmith Jack', and two in the winter of 1738 against an unbeaten coachman, by the name of William Slann, and Joseph Parsons, a lighterman. In June of the following year he was advertised to meet the prolific Irish champion Patrick Henley, another early boxer who deserves to be better remembered if only for the large number of bouts in which he participated. The Dublin hero was undefeated at the time of their meeting but Boswell boasted that, since he was "famous for breaking Men's Jaws", Henley would imminently be requiring the services of a surgeon. In late 1740 the 'Terrible Tom-Boy', Richard Foster, and the 'Terrible Welchman', James Francis, were lined up as Boswell opponents and, for an intended match on 31 March 1741, Peter Brookes, a fellow chairman, was selected to be his antagonist. Other proposed bouts for Boswell during that year featured James Taylor, a veteran waterman, and John Cooper, a Somerset man who had previously repelled all contenders in his native county. The former would, undoubtedly, have been an awkward foe since he had beaten 'Hammersmith Jack' and the conqueror of the 'Venetian Gondolier', the Lincolnshire drover John Whitacre (later wrongly referred to as Bob Whitaker), as well as drawing with the renowned Thomas Allen ("vulgarly call'd Pipes"). During August 1742 an unbeaten Suffolk pugilist, Robert Smith, was announced as challenging the "famous Mr. Boswell", whilst an apparently long-awaited encounter with a coachman called William Flanderkin was publicized for 27 July 1743.

However, of all the advertised contests involving Boswell, for which no results are available in extant newspapers, perhaps the most interesting was the one at Broughton's Amphitheatre in November 1745 against Thomas Hawksley, a massive Derbyshire life-guardsman, who reputedly weighed in the region of 17 stone. Since Pugnus asserted that the gypsy scarcely tipped the scales at 11 stone, the physical disparity between the men must have been extremely marked. It is difficult to imagine today a fighter of Boswell's size prepared to concede such weight (even if a boxing authority existed which was foolhardy enough to allow it) but two hundred and fifty years ago the difference was not considered a major issue. This is even better illustrated by the fact that Hawksley fought the celebrated Ned Hunt, a boxer well known to have been little more than half his weight. Hunt's surprising victory over his gigantic adversary emphasized his unquestionable talents whilst simultaneously exposing Hawksley's somewhat limited ability. It would, therefore, be safe to say that Boswell's match-up with the life-guardsman was not as dangerous an undertaking as it may at first have appeared. Indeed a riskier proposition might well have been Jack James who, although lighter, was anxious "to try Art and Agility against Weight and Superior Force" in August 1746. James, whose father is supposedly depicted by Hogarth in 'The March to Finchley', was highly regarded as a pugilist and had previously been billed as the "bravest of his Age in the manly Art of Boxing". More difficult still would have been the aforementioned Jack Slack, who was scheduled to meet Boswell in December 1748, just 16 months before the former's famous victory over Broughton. (In fact Slack definitely seems to have beaten Boswell at some point as the *Daily Advertiser* commented on this in January 1750 when announcing one of Jack's bouts with George Taylor.)

After his milling career was over, Boswell soon disappeared into obscurity. He may have returned to the life of a gypsy, but it is highly probable that he resorted to the profession of highwayman on a more regular basis. It was certainly rumoured that, in the latter capacity, he preyed on travellers between Hounslow Heath and the Oxford Road. If this was the case, he was apparently lucky enough not to have suffered the same unfortunate fate as his former opponent, James Field.

The Fighting Miller from Hadley

A T   M R .   B R O U G H T O N ' S Amphitheatre in Oxford-Road, on Wednesday next, the 26th instant, will be a severe Trial of Manhood between the following Champions.

I JOSEPH LINE, from Hadley in Hertfordshire, where I am the Terror of all around, having fought and beat the best Men the County could produce; not content, hearing of the extraordinary Feats of Mr. John James, was determined to give him Battle; for which Purpose I am come to London, well back'd, for considerable Sums, by those who are Judges of both our Abilities. I, therefore, do hereby invite Mr. James to meet and fight me, at the Time and Place, above, for Ten Guineas, when Gentlemen may depend on seeing a good Battle, on my Part, equall'd by few, and excell'd by none.

Joseph Line

I JOHN JAMES am at Mr. Line's Service, and will not fail meeting him agreeable to his Invitation, and comply with all its Circumstances, as Time, Place, and Sum, when I shall oblige him to repent his rash Undertaking, and submit to my superior Skill and Judgment.

John James

Note, There will be several Bye-Battles, as usual. The Doors will be open'd at Three, and the Champions mount at Five.

The above notice, from the *Daily Advertiser* of 22 August 1747, appears to announce the London début of a fighting miller from Hadley, Joseph Line(s). (Although he stated that he hailed from Hertfordshire, it must be presumed that the Hadley mentioned is the one in close proximity to Barnet, which was then in Middlesex but sometimes erroneously considered to be in the county of Hertfordshire.) Apparently, by this time, Line had earned a considerable reputation in the local vicinity and felt confident enough in his abilities to invite one of the premier pugilists to set to with him. Jack James was certainly a daunting test for any ambitious aspirant for pugilistic fame and, unsurprisingly, on the day the Hadley man's audacious sortie ended in disappointment. Line blamed his defeat, "after a very severe Battle", on the ineptitude of his second. However, the same reason, along with accidental falls and various unlucky injuries, was frequently given by many boxers to explain away their losses.

Convinced that he had benefited from the experience, and bolstered by George Taylor's promise to second him, Line challenged James to a return contest for £20, to take place on 14 October of the same year. Whether he was more successful on this occasion is not known, but, whatever the result, he does not seem to have returned to Broughton's Amphitheatre until July 1748 when he was billed as meeting Ned Hunt for ten guineas. Hunt, who six months earlier had advised his prospective protagonist, William Cutts, "to bring his Coffin with him", showed more respect towards Line yet nevertheless boasted that his latest adversary would submit to his greater expertise. Although the outcome of the affair again remains obscure, it is difficult to envisage the seasoned and adroit Hunt succumbing to a man who had previously participated in so few stage battles.

A period of over three and a half years appears to have elapsed before Line once more performed in the metropolis. There is no way of being certain, however, since evidence exists of Broughton organizing matches which were not publicized in the newspapers but instead, presumably, by handbills and word of mouth. Alternatively, Line may have moved from Hadley and been the "Joseph Line of Hitchin, miller" who was indicted and detained in 1750 for a triple assault. Certainly, his later advertisements made no mention of Hadley, merely stating that he came from Hertfordshire.

In keeping with Line's policy of contending with pugilists of proven quality, his two advertised encounters for March 1752 both featured men who had beaten Ned Hunt. The first was against Thomas Cook, originally from Cheltenham, who at this period was living in Goswell Street, where Mr Pickwick later lodged with Mrs Bardell in Charles Dickens's *The Pickwick Papers*. Besides the prestige gained by having "defeated the celebrated Mr. Hunt with Ease", Cook could also claim a win over Joe James, brother of the now deceased Jack James. Joshua Hawkins, an inhabitant of Cow Cross, a notoriously insalubrious location not far from Smithfield Market, provided stern competition for the second bout. In a stage-fighting career dating back at least eight years, Hawkins had overcome the challenge of Hunt no less than four times. Just two months previously he had fought a very "tight Battle" with the famed boxer-cricketer Tom Faulkener.

Despite the calibre of the opposition, the interest in Line's advertised activities of spring 1752 lies not so much in the contests themselves but in the actual venue. This was categorically stated as being Broughton's Amphitheatre at a date nearly two years after most historians insist the establishment had been shut down. It is generally believed that a piqued Duke of Cumberland, Broughton's backer, used his considerable influence to bring about the closure shortly after his man's defeat by Slack in April 1750. However, such an assumption is obviously patently wrong. Indeed it was still open in May 1753 when, according to an announcement in the *Daily Advertiser*, the "Battle which was to have been fought this Day [2nd] at Mr. Broughton's Amphitheatre, between John Slack and Thomas Faulkener, is, by the Desire of several Gentlemen, put off".

Line himself was not billed to appear at Broughton's Amphitheatre again. Whether this was because fewer bouts were advertised in the newspapers at that time, or because he curtailed his prize-fighting career, it is not possible to ascertain.

Cudgels Expert Felled by Local Pugilist

The first known bareknuckle contest actually held in Barnet was that between an Irishman by the name of Nicholas Grady and a local pugilist called Perkinson. The powerfully built Grady had an excellent reputation with the cudgels but, despite his pre-fight claims, his expertise apparently did not extend to fisticuffs. Perkinson, who was considerably lighter, was nicknamed the 'little Barnet poulterer' and plied his trade as a higgler in London's Fleet

Market. (Situated between Fleet Street and Holborn, the market was surprisingly modern in concept and consisted of two rows of single-storey shops connected by a covered walkway with skylights.)

The two men met on Barnet Common in September 1761 when, in a bruising battle, the underdog showed up the deficiencies of his much heavier opponent. Grady's backer, Dennis O'Kelly, is supposed to have lost the then considerable sum of £600 on the fight while the victorious Perkinson happily walked away with upwards of 200 guineas. This he used to purchase a public house in the Old Street area of the metropolis.

Shepherd Metes Out Punishment to Butcher

No further mention can be found for local mills until some ten years later when Jack Shepherd (not to be confused with the thief captured on Finchley Common) and Charles Coant were matched at Barnet in February or April 1771. The latter was a butcher in London's close-knit Clare Market, which specialized in meat and fish and had been established over one hundred years earlier. The former was referred to in *Boxiana* as "a Shepherd of some experience" and the author also commented that he "knew how to manage a flock". However, this is possibly an example of Egan's occasional facetiousness since *Pancratia* and the 'Chronological History of Boxing' (contained in the November 1797 issue of the *Sporting Magazine*) stated that Shepherd was a baker. Unfortunately, none of the above sources described the contest in any detail but all references to the affair agreed that it was extremely hard-fought. It appears that Shepherd emerged the victor after 35 minutes, although Egan is less precise about the exact time than other historians.

Shepherd's only other documented fight, a win over the capable Jack Lamb, suggests that he was a boxer of no mean ability. One might have expected him, therefore, to have had an easier time against Coant since the butcher is said to have bragged that he had participated in 21 bouts and lost them all. This viewpoint, however, is probably rather harsh. There may have been no truth in Coant's boast, and since he was reputed to have encountered good-calibre opposition, his possible lamentable record was very likely not an accurate reflection of his true worth. He certainly provided a severe test for Tom Juchau in the paviour's first important battle (13 June 1764), and Juchau, with his defeat of George Milsom the next year, could be considered to have had a valid claim to the title of champion.

It is interesting that the *Public Advertiser* of 16 June 1764 thought that Coant died the night following his meeting with Juchau but then some early newspapers were prone to dispatch fighters rather prematurely. Another good example of this tendency can be found the decade before when the *Daily Advertiser* noted George Taylor's demise as occurring on 21 February 1750. The same journal, during the summer of that year, then printed advertisements for cricket matches involving Tom Faulkener at "Mr. George Taylor's, the Fountain at Deptford".

'Death' at Barnet

One of the renowned Stephen Oliver's few recorded bouts took place at Barnet in 1776 against a butcher by the name of William Small. Oliver was known by the grim sobriquet of 'Death' but this nickname did not have any sinister connotations, being bestowed on the pugilist because of his bloodless pallor during contests. A well-built man, never exceeding 12 stone in weight, he was a favourite of Jack Broughton who considered him one of the best teachers and exponents of his boxing system. He participated, according to Oxberry, in more battles than any man in England and often defied the odds against much heavier opponents. Egan described the meeting at Barnet as being for £20 and observed that "Death very soon proved too much for Small". He did not mention any date but Miles was of the opinion that it occurred on 3 July 1776.

In *Pugilistica* he printed an epigram which apparently had appeared in a diurnal of the time and went as follows:

> *Ah! foolish wight, why strive to conquer Death?*
> *When he, thou know'st can stop the vital breath;*
> *That ruthless tyrant rules the lives of all,*
> *And vanquishes the Great, as well as Small.*

Newspapers such as the *Gazetteer and New Daily Advertiser*, the *Morning Chronicle and London Advertiser*, the *Morning Post and Daily Advertiser* and the *Public Advertiser* all had no mention of the Oliver–Small mill taking place during July 1776. However, on Thursday 8 August the *Public Advertiser* did report a conflict which happened on the Tuesday "on the Course at Barnet for forty guineas between a man called the bruising Butcher and a Carpenter by the name of Death". It further remarked that the match was fought in front of an estimated 4000 people, including 600 butchers, and continued for 15 minutes before the carpenter received a foul blow that put an end to proceedings.

A similar account was contained in the *Middlesex Journal and Evening Advertiser* but, to complicate matters further, *Lloyds Evening Post and British Chronicle* of 7-9 August had a slightly different version. This newspaper described a pitched battle at Barnet, on the Tuesday, involving the same combatants but for 20 guineas and with 'Death' administering the foul blow. It stated that Oliver's opponent came from Fleet Market, which was in accordance with an assertion in the *Sporting Magazine's* 'Chronological History of Boxing' that Small plied his trade in that area. That two butchers from the same market should meet 'Death' at Barnet within a month of each other seems unlikely. However, whether these contests were one and the same, or perhaps two involving Small, must remain open to conjecture.

The next year, on 16 July 1777, Oliver once more fought a butcher at Barnet, his adversary on this occasion being one Allen from Clare Market. The encounter, for 20 guineas a side, was won by "the noted Death" in "near fifteen minutes". Although three contemporary newspapers carried details of the meeting, again there is a discrepancy in that the *Public Advertiser* thought that the contest did not take place, reporting that "when the time arrived Mr. Death refused to fight".

Oliver, supposed to have been active since the days of Broughton, was regarded as a veteran at the time of his Barnet appearances. Nevertheless he continued to box for some time afterwards. It is believed that his last bout occurred in April 1788 when he was beaten at Blackheath by the powerful Jewish fighter, Elisha Crabbe. He was still living in 1793 but thereafter no trace can be found of him.

The Mysterious Peter Bath

Peter Bath defeated William Allen, a Clare Market butcher (almost certainly the one who met Stephen Oliver the following year), in a well-fought contest on 20 August 1776. According to the 'Annals of Pugilism', contained in a book said to have been written by the eminent prize-fighter Richard Humphries (occasionally Humphreys), Bath's occupation was that of postboy. However, the *Sporting Magazine's* 'Chronological History of Boxing' described him as a smith and "long the hero of Bristol". His opponent, so the same source related, had emerged successful in many unrecorded battles. Their meeting at Barnet lasted 40 minutes, but no additional details are available.

Bath's subsequent career is also shrouded in mystery, except for a win over Joe Hood in September 1778 and a loss to Bill Purdue when the Bristol fighter was at the veteran stage. The victory over Hood, even allowing for his opponent's then supposedly indifferent health, does give some indication of Bath's capabilities. Hood had overcome some noted performers and twice competed creditably against champion Harry Sellers. As for Bath's defeat by Purdue, this was certainly no disgrace as the latter was reputedly never beaten during an extensive career.

On retiring, Bath did not entirely sever his links with the prize-ring. He umpired a marathon four-and-a-half-hour match in September 1790, and soon afterwards seconded a brass founder in a much shorter affair at Kentish Town. It is clear that he was rated amongst the premier boxers of his time since *The Star* (7 May 1799) named him as being one of the "celebrated pugilists" attending the St Giles funeral of the notorious 'Tinman', Bill Hooper.

The Remarkable Bill Purdue

The aforementioned lightweight phenomenon, Bill Purdue, appeared at least twice at Barnet during the early 1780s. Purdue, born in January 1758, was barely 5 feet tall and weighed just 8 stone 12 pounds, but this did not prevent him from taking on and beating men considerably larger than himself. He originally served as a sailor in both the East and West Indies trade, and also spent nine months on board a man-of-war before returning home to become a butcher in Fleet Market. His initial bout in Barnet was also his first contest of note and took place on the common, against Ben Hamilton, for ten guineas a side. In this instance the 'little fighting butcher', as Purdue was called, did not concede any weight. However, he was up against an extremely confident opponent who was highly rated as a boxer. In the opinion of Humphries' 'Annals of Pugilism' the two were equally matched but Purdue succeeded in taking the lead and did not relinquish it, winning in 30 minutes.

The full date of the Hamilton fight is not known but it is generally believed to have been in 1781. Purdue's other mill in the area, against one Mintam, was also chronicled by both Humphries' 'Annals' and *Fistiana* as being fought in the same year, but this is possibly an error since there is no doubt that the two met on Barnet Common in 1783. Perhaps they had more than one encounter at Barnet, although there do not appear to be any existing contemporary reports to substantiate the earlier date, whereas at least three accounts have survived for a bout occurring on Tuesday 7 October 1783.

Although it comes as no surprise to find variations in the details given, all these sources agreed that Mintam, a butcher originating from Newgate Market, proved a worthy adversary for the "noted" Purdue. Indeed, according to the *Public Advertiser*, he dominated the first 15 minutes of the action and Purdue's supporters deemed it necessary to break into the ring in order to give their man time to recover his wind. The delay obviously proved beneficial to Purdue since "on the second Onset, after a Contest of about twenty Minutes, he was declared Victorious". The *St. James's Chronicle or British Evening-Post* and the *Morning Post and Daily Advertiser* described the affair as a desperate one with the first 20 minutes being especially severe. They also gave the victory to Purdue, but not until 1 hour and 10 minutes of action had elapsed. Both papers commented on the great number of spectators present, the *Morning Post* adding that "more blackguards were never assembled on a similar occasion". A further newspaper, the *Whitehall Evening-Post*, asserted that the "terrible conflict" took place at Barnet, for ten guineas, on 6 October. Purdue's opponent was not named but he was said to have been a butcher living at the Cock-in-the-Corner, Ludgate Street. Again, Purdue was credited with a win, the length of the bout being given as one and a half hours.

Purdue continued to thrive after these engagements. If Egan is correct, he was involved in the remarkable number of at least 100 battles and turn-ups without once suffering the indignity of defeat. This may be more feasible than it sounds since the *Public Advertiser* of 2 October 1784, covering Purdue's confrontation at Brentford with a buckle-cutter named Tom Chant (Chaunt), emphasized his exceptional defensive dexterity.

There is also a possibility that Purdue had another link with Barnet. He may have been the William Purdoe of Fleet Market who, in 1780, served "the poor of the parish with good and wholesome beef with some mutton and beef sewet [*sic*] occasionally at and for the sum of eighteen pence per stone". (Discrepancies in the spelling of names were prevalent in the 18th century. The pugilist was actually referred to as "Purdoe" in the *Public Advertiser* report of the Mintam fight and "Purdue" in the later Chant one. Equally, Mintam has been recorded as 'Mintum', 'Minton' and even 'Winton'.)

It is mentioned in *Boxiana* that Purdue was still very much alive in 1821 and continuing to trade in Fleet Market where he was a respected master butcher. At this time he had been married some 35 years and brought up 14 children.

Towers Has His Day

On 22 November 1784, bricklayer Bill Towers took on the accomplished Bill Day for 50 guineas a side. Like Peter Bath, Day could claim a win over Joe Hood and was referred to by Miles as "an active and game pugilist". The match was originally to have taken place at an inn-yard in Barnet but, following magisterial interference, the location was switched to the nearby race-ground. The *Barnet Gazette* of 3 July 1858, in one of a series of articles looking back on local history, mentioned this as being on the common "in close proximity to the Well, viz. around the spot now called Whiting's Hill".

Sporting historian Dennis Brailsford commented in *Sport, Time & Society* that race-courses such as the one at Barnet were ideal fight venues since they were outside the town. They were also likely to have a grandstand, however basic, from which affluent spectators could observe the entertainment in comparative comfort. With regard to Barnet, there is little doubt that he is correct about the favourable position, at least until the enclosure of the common lands in 1815 which led to the races being transferred to the vicinity of Barnet Hill. However, whether or not there was a grandstand is more difficult to verify although, in view of the high regard in which the race-ground was held at the time, it is possible that one existed.

The Day–Towers contest seems to have attracted much attention and the *Gazetteer and New Daily Advertiser* noted that a large number of people had assembled by two o'clock. Forty-five minutes later the boxers made their appearance on the rapidly constructed 30-foot stage. Day was seconded by one Will Gallant whilst his antagonist had the benefit of advice from his brother, fellow bruiser Jack Towers, who would also fight at Barnet in the future. Hostilities commenced with Day being the clear favourite and, for the first ten minutes, this was reflected in the odds being bandied about at ringside. However, according to *Boxiana*, Day, having boasted of an easy victory, was so confident of success that he made the fatal mistake of severely underestimating his opponent. In due course, so Egan described, Towers showed him the error of his ways. Trapping his cocksure adversary in a corner, the bricklayer held him firmly with one hand and pummelled him heavily with the other. There was now evidently no way back into the bout for the battered Day and, after 33 minutes, the underdog secured an unexpected triumph.

Egan's account does appear to be somewhat at variance with a report in the *Public Advertiser* of 24 November. This implied that the affair, which it said lasted upwards of 35 minutes, was a considerably more even contest with both men sustaining severe damage, especially about the head. Furthermore, the newspaper was of the opinion that the meeting had been "the most obstinately fought battle within the memory of man". This view was backed up by the recollections of an old sportsman (strangely enough reprinted in one of Egan's anecdotal compilations) who had witnessed the occasion. He remembered that "the English claret had flowed so freely, that never before or since, did I see two men so thoroughly and handsomely painted with the true blood red, from the crown of the head to the waistband".

Bill Towers was another 18th-century pugilist about whom little is known. Dowling only listed the above fight for Towers in *Fistiana*, and other ring historians appear unaware of any further activity on his part. Nevertheless he did have at least one more success. On 1 January 1788, the *Morning Post and Daily Advertiser* reported that the day previously he had defeated a fellow bricklayer by the name of Knowles in a spirited encounter lasting about 20 minutes. As for Bill Day, Egan would have us believe that he died shortly after his bout with Towers from the effects of the relentless punishment inflicted upon him during their confrontation. No evidence, however, can be found to support this assertion.

Barnet Welcomes its First Champion

The first champion to exhibit his skills in the Barnet area was Tom Johnson, real name Jackling, a corn-porter from Derby whom Egan erroneously described as coming from Yorkshire. A contemporary publication, *The Complete Art of Boxing* by An Amateur of Eminence, commented in 1788 that Johnson "by fair fighting is the only successor in the athletic art to Mr. Broughton, as he stands to his man much upon the same plan as that excellent master". It was Johnson who was responsible for bringing back respectability to the championship of England after a dark period during which fixed fights, or 'crosses', were prevalent. The date, however, when he was first recognized as holding this high honour is unclear. Egan and Miles were both of the opinion that Johnson's contest in 1787 with Bill Ward (wrongly referred to after the 18th century as Warr) firmly established him as champion. Humphries' 'Annals of Pugilism' maintained the position was denied him for a further two years. Either way it must be borne in mind that the title was purely an unofficial one since, unlike today, there were no governing bodies in existence to invigilate.

Johnson's opponent at Barnet, for 50 guineas, was Bill Love, who, Humphries' 'Annals' stated, came from the Bristol School of Pugilism. (The *Sporting Magazine's* 'Chronological History of Boxing' described him as a Whitechapel butcher.) The bout may have occurred on 11 January 1786, or possibly a day or two later, but it is not recorded in extant newspapers. *Boxiana* related that it lasted a mere five minutes, by which time Love was "so completely cut up as to leave Johnson in possession of the ground". The calibre of Tom's performance can be judged by the fact that Love subsequently defeated George Ring, the well-respected baker from Bath.

During the same month Johnson returned to Barnet to face the aforementioned Jack Towers. Although the latter was credited by the *Sporting Magazine* with wins over "Love, Death and all who had before opposed him", he proved unable to prevent Johnson from registering another victory. However, Egan appears mistaken in writing that Towers quickly surrendered since the *Whitehall Evening-Post* declared the "severe battle" was of a 43-minute duration. No date was given in *Boxiana* for the confrontation but *Pugilistica, Fistiana* and Humphries' 'Annals' all incorrectly opted for February 1786. It actually took place on 23 January for £50 a side and, as expected, "great bets were depending on the occasion". An interesting little anecdote then appeared in both the *Public Advertiser* and the *London Chronicle* at the beginning of February:

Johnson, who fought and beat Towers a few days ago at Barnet, lately performed the following extraordinary feat of strength. Placing three sacks of grain one upon another, he took the uppermost, and throwing it on his shoulder, hopped with it three times round, and then clear over the other two sacks.

The next January came Johnson's affair with Ward which, despite an unsatisfactory conclusion, established his supremacy as the country's premier pugilist. On 12 October of the same year he was scheduled to fight once more at Barnet against the hard-hitting Irishman Michael Ryan but the report of an imminent press-gang raid caused the bout to be deferred. (Press-gangs were bands of armed men led by the King's officers who crimped unsuspecting bystanders into service in the Navy during the 18th and early 19th centuries. They were, in effect, little more than kidnappers and were even known to carry off a bridegroom and congregation from the church door.) With regard to the postponement, the *Daily Universal Register* delighted in commenting that "perhaps, this is the first time British tars ever prevented a battle". When the encounter happened later at Wraysbury the loser Ryan complained, apparently with some justification, of the strong partiality shown to his opponent. Johnson repeated his success in their subsequent rematch before registering his finest win by overcoming the remarkably strong Birmingham hero, Isaac Perrins, on 22 October 1789 in a meeting which greatly excited the imagination of the contemporary press.

On 17 January 1791, Johnson faced the challenge of the Bristolian Ben Bryan (t) or Briant, commonly known as 'Big Ben' at the time, and as Ben Brain by later chroniclers. It proved to be Johnson's final contest and, at Wrotham in Kent, he was forced to bow to the superiority of his determined antagonist. Whilst his demeanour as champion had been exemplary, his conduct after retirement left much to be desired and he appears to have become involved with the underworld community. A contemporary notorious criminal, John Wiltshire, who was hanged in July 1793 for highway robbery, stated that the ex-bruiser knew of all the recent acts of larceny that had been committed. On one occasion, at least, it is known that he was apprehended (with great difficulty) for a pickpocketing offence, but was later discharged from

Chelmsford gaol, "no bill being found against him". It was Johnson's propensity for gambling that played a major part in his slide into ignominy and also contributed to his failure as a publican. He ultimately suffered the indignity of losing the licences of public houses in Duke Street, Lincoln's Inn Fields and Cooper Alley, Dublin. On 21 January 1797, just six years after his last ring appearance, he died a pauper in Ireland.

Johnson's demise elicited little attention and the following brief notice of death in a Dublin newspaper, *Saunders's News-Letter and Daily Advertiser*, typified the general lack of interest: "... at Phibbiborough [*sic*], after a short illness, Mr. Thomas Johnson, the noted English pugilist; he fought sixteen stage battles, and never was subdued but once".

Royalty on the Common

We now come to Daniel Mendoza, the celebrated Jewish champion and one of the most accomplished boxers ever to grace the prize-ring. Mendoza stood only 5 feet 7 inches tall and often found himself at a considerable physical disadvantage, but used his agility and speed to great effect during a spectacular and colourful career. According to his autobiography, he was born in Aldgate, East London, on 5 July 1764, although most historians give the date as being the previous year. However, in the De Paiba Circumcision Register the date of 12 July 1765 is entered as the day of the circumcision of Daniel, son of Abraham Mendoza. As Daniel's father is known to have been Abraham, and as Jewish boys are usually circumcised eight days after birth, the most likely date seems to be 4 (possibly 5) July 1765. Further support for the year 1765 can be found in a book by the son of the first Marquess of Reading, who recorded the statesman's grandmother, Sarah, as being Daniel's niece.

Mendoza first went to Barnet in January 1786 to attend the Tom Johnson–Bill Love bout (see page 33), although he remembered this as being some three years earlier. He was apparently disappointed at the brevity of the fight but described in his memoirs, which he wrote in middle-age, how he himself provided some fierce action for those onlookers who witnessed his participation in two impromptu encounters in the area. These occurred during his journey back to town, the first lasting nearly an hour and the second, with a butcher at Finchley, 30 minutes. Both times Mendoza emerged victorious and well rewarded due to the generosity of two sporting gentlemen and subscriptions raised from the gathered spectators.

At the instigation of the Prince of Wales, later George IV, Mendoza returned to Barnet on 17 April 1787 to contend against Sam Martin, the noted 'Bath Butcher'. (Here again his recollections can be disputed for Daniel was of the opinion that their well-chronicled meeting took place in 1785.) Martin had already built up a good reputation in the West Country before going to the metropolis. He can be found on 31 May 1785 defeating a coal-heaver behind Bedford House before vanquishing a Rotherhithe baker at Sevenoaks some three months later. The next year he performed creditably, albeit unsuccessfully, against Richard Humphries at Newmarket. Fellow pugilist Tom Fewtrell considered Martin an unfair fighter ("he practices every manoeuvre, and takes every mean advantage that is possible") but did concede that the 'Bath Butcher' was a strong and accurate puncher.

Mendoza recounted that he and Martin had previously been matched to set to at Shepherds Bush, but this was prevented on the order of a magistrate by a party of the Prince of Wales's own 10th Regiment of Dragoons. His Royal Highness, however, was not to be denied his pleasure and the affair was accordingly rearranged, although some attempt was made to keep the venue secret. Indeed the *Morning Herald* of 16 April 1787 commented that "though both Barnet and Finchley have been proposed, it is yet uncertain where the contest will take place, the persons interested in the event thereof being adverse to mentioning the spot, lest the sport of the day should be interrupted by the interference of the magistracy".

At twenty minutes past three the combatants mounted a specially built stage on Barnet Race-course and prepared themselves for battle in front of an audience of 5000, which included both the Prince of Wales and his brother, the Duke of York. In the supporting role for Mendoza were Tom Johnson and Tom Tring, a porter at the Prince's residence, Carlton House. Ben Bryan, together with Bob Packer, seconded Martin.

The well-built Bath bruiser was installed as favourite due to the prevailing opinion that he was the more powerful hitter. However, as the *Gazetteer and New Daily Advertiser* was at pains to point out, since "falling without a knock-down stroke was barred, Martin, who is dextrous in this play, was therefore deprived of his best resource". Not surprisingly, in view of his adversary's later achievements, the butcher was unable to cope with the skill and speed of the scientific Mendoza. He was forced to yield after a hard struggle which was acknowledged to be one of the best seen since the days of Jack Broughton.

2. Daniel Mendoza, the eminent Jewish fistic hero, who fought with Sam Martin at Barnet before the Prince of Wales.

The various contemporary newspapers that covered the day's activities did not agree on the fight's length but it was certainly between 20 and 31 minutes. Mendoza himself thought 26 minutes to be correct. Whatever the truth of the matter, there can be no doubt that it was considerably quicker than Humphries' defeat of Martin, a fact which greatly increased the former's intense dislike of the Jewish boxer. There was a similar discrepancy in the reporting the next day of the two combatants' condition at the end of the contest. The *Daily Universal Register* stated that "they were both much beaten" whilst the *World, Fashionable Advertiser* described the victor as being so little hurt that "he leaped on the railing of the scaffold, which was nearly two yards from the ground". Martin was certainly heavily punished – he had to be carried from the scene and was taken to the Red Lion in Barnet where his wounds were dressed.

"The great personage", as Mendoza called the royal patron for this occasion, was obviously highly delighted with the East-Ender's performance for he afterwards presented him with a sum amounting to "nearly five hundred pounds" in addition to the £50 he had given him before the bout. The future King's enthusiasm for prize-fighting was a significant factor in the sport experiencing a

*3. A cartoon by the renowned caricaturist James Gillray of the Prince of Wales,
later George IV, an ardent supporter of the prize-ring.*

resurgence of interest such as had not been evident since the
Broughton era. Between 1786 and 1788 he attended several
matches but vowed never to do so again after witnessing the death
of the unfortunate bruiser Earl at the hands of Tom Tyne, the tailor,
on Brighton Race-ground. Although most historians believe he kept
his word, Miles remained sceptical; he was right to be so as *The
Times*, less than two years after the Earl tragedy, reported the Prince
attending a battle in Hyde Park between one Chapman and a noted
Jew. Indeed, his links with pugilism continued well into the next

century for, prior to his coronation, on 19 July 1821, he commissioned John Jackson to appoint 18 leading prize-fighters to keep order during the ceremony at Westminster Abbey.

Having witnessed Mendoza's triumph, the Prince rode off but many of the crowd stayed to watch a second mill between Doyle, a sailor, and a soldier named Mutton. During the 45-minute bout the former suffered a severe eye injury but was still able to register a well-deserved win over an opponent who, in the latter stages, dropped several times without being hit.

To return to Mendoza, he was beaten by his bitter adversary Richard Humphries the following January, but subsequently twice avenged this setback and also recorded two wins over the Bristolian Bill Ward. His career at the highest level came to an end on 15 April 1795 at the hands of 'Gentleman' John Jackson. Later the commander-in-chief of the sport, Jackson was probably more renowned in that role and as a professor of pugilism (amongst his pupils was Lord Byron) than for his three prize-ring appearances. Against Mendoza he certainly failed to live up to his cognomen. His ungentlemanly conduct – holding his antagonist's hair with one hand and hitting him with the other – did little to help the outweighed champion's fortunes. After this loss, the manner of which incensed him greatly, Mendoza concentrated his energies on sparring tours around the major towns of the United Kingdom and also ran a public house in Whitechapel. He only entered the ring on two further occasions, conquering Harry Lee in 1806 and losing to fellow veteran Tom Owen 14 years later.

In a letter in the *Oracle, and the Daily Advertiser* of 5 December 1801, Mendoza stated that he had been involved in 32 pitched battles whilst *Bell's Life in London* later placed the final figure at 38. However, his true record prior to the Martin fight cannot be substantiated since the names mentioned by Mendoza in his early career are, with the exception of Tom Tyne, virtually unchronicled. Apart from Humphries, Jackson and Owen, the only other occasion he is believed to have been beaten was by Tyne in a bout Daniel recalled as taking place in 1783. (A loss to "a taylor" can be found in the *Public Advertiser* of 10 November 1785. It is possible that this could be the same contest bearing in mind the fighter's memory for dates was, as has been seen, now and then suspect, but equally it could be a further unrecognized defeat.)

What cannot be disputed, though, was Mendoza's unsurpassed insight into the theories of boxing, which was amply demonstrated many times to the gratification of the thousands who had the pleasure of seeing him perform.

During an address at a Fives Court benefit in August 1820, the ever-modest Mendoza declared: "I think I have the right to call myself the Father of the Science". It is a claim few would dispute. He died in Horseshoe Alley, Petticoat Lane, London, on 3 September 1836. His eminence can be gauged by the fact that, according to Paul H Emden, at least 25 portraits were produced of him and his battles and seven medals struck in his honour. Emden, writing in his book *Jews of Britain*, considered that this made Mendoza "the most popular figure in Jewry".

4. An entry from Daniel Mendoza's cash book / diary recording the election to parliament of the renowned former prize-fighter, John Gully. (Reproduced by kind permission of Michael Taggart and Harry Mendoza.)

Court Edict on Barnet Pitched Battles

There can be little doubt that unreported contests at Barnet between anonymous bruisers were far from infrequent during the latter part of the 18th century. In fact, in August 1889 the *Barnet Press*, writing about the town during the coaching age, emphasized the existence of such activities whilst commenting on the lack of morality among the lower classes of the time. According to this source, "it was no unusual thing to see a pugilistic encounter in the public streets – men stripped to the waist fighting, for perhaps half-an-hour or more, without any interference".

By 1787 the situation regarding the occurrence of indiscriminate milling in and around Barnet seems to have become a serious enough matter of concern for the Court of the Liberty of St Albans to issue an edict aimed at eradicating the problem. The Quarter Sessions roll for the Easter term of that year shows that during April the court advised the county's Justices of the Peace to attend and prevent all proposed local "pitched Battles". Every High Constable was also instructed to be present in order to assist the Justices in the execution of their duty. The court further directed that this decree should appear in the London newspapers and "a sufficient Number of Copies thereof printed and stuck up in all public Places near to the said Town of Barnett [*sic*]". The first part of the order was certainly carried out for the following is taken from a notice which was placed in the *General Evening Post* one month later:

INFORMATION having been given to this Court, that large numbers of people have lately, and at different times, assembled together at or near the town of Chipping-Barnet; in the liberty of Saint Alban, for the purpose of Fighting Pitched Battles; and that more such Meetings are intended, which the Justices of the Peace for the said liberty intend to prevent: This Court, considering that all such unlawful assemblies occasion great Riots, Tumults and Disorders, wherever they are held, and that they tend much to disturb the public peace, doth recommend to his Majesty's Justices of the Peace for this County to attend wherever such Meetings may be, within this County, for the purpose of preventing the like evil: And to that end, this Court doth expressly order and direct all High Constables of this County to attend upon every occasion, with their respective Petty Constables, that they may be ready to aid and assist such Justices in the Execution of their office, if thereunto required.

Coal-Porters Substitute at Finchley

5. Bristolian Ben Bryan (Brain),
Tom Johnson's great rival.

A hand injury, sustained by one of the protagonists when he was thrown out of his one-horse chaise, prevented the contest between the 'Tinman', Bill Hooper, and Cotterell, a shoemaker, from going ahead at Finchley on 14 August 1789. However, the spectators refused to forgo their entertainment and two coal-porters were therefore matched to provide the day's sport. Both men, while blessed with tremendous physical strength, were considerably lacking in skill. Consequently their one-and-a-half-hour battle exhibited much ferocity but little science and, as their blows were so heavy, they finished covered with wounds.

The occasion was only made memorable by the accidental meeting of Tom Johnson and his great rival Ben Bryan. At this chance encounter the former signalled an immediate challenge by throwing his hat in the air and, when Bryan answered likewise, they stripped ready for action. It was only the interference of their concerned friends that prevented them from contending on the spot. They reluctantly agreed, therefore, to get together the following morning when they signed articles to fight, as the *Whitehall Evening-Post* reported, "some day previous to 20th October next", for 100 guineas a side. However, for various reasons, they were not destined to oppose each other until their aforementioned battle of January 1791, which was the last time either entered the ring in a fighting capacity.

Cobbler Nailed by the 'Tinman'

Tom Johnson again visited Barnet on 5 September 1789, on this occasion seconding the fearless Bristolian tinker, Bill Hooper. The 'Tinman', born in 1766, was about 5 feet 7 $1/2$ inches in height, weighed approximately 11 stone and had a reputation as a determined and courageous bruiser. He attracted a considerable crowd for his rescheduled contest with Cotterell, which took place on the common for ten guineas a side. The shoemaker was attended by an old adversary of Johnson, Bill Ward, who was later much in demand in the capacity of second and looked after such champions as Daniel Mendoza, Jem Belcher, Henry Pearce and Tom Cribb.

Three days after the fight, the *Diary; or, Woodfall's Register* reported that "no stage was erected, but stakes drove into the ground, and cords run round them". At around three o'clock the combatants set to. Their fiercely fought confrontation of 18 rounds lasted about 35 minutes at which point Hooper, showing very few marks of battle, was declared the winner. However, his opponent, felled 16 times, accepted his punishment manfully and, according to the *Oracle Bell's New World* of 10 September 1789, "it was universally acknowledged that had he been equal to the Tinman in skill, he would have beat him". The Barnet encounter was not to be the only time the two faced up to one another. They are later listed in advertisements in *The Times* as participating in sparring demonstrations at the Lyceum in the Strand on 2 and 16 April 1791 and at Panton Street, Haymarket, during May of the same year.

A bruiser referred to as the 'Tinman' is mentioned in the *Oracle Bell's New World* as scheduled to meet a brickmaker at Finchley on 29 September 1789. This is most likely to have been Hooper, but unfortunately neither this nor any other newspaper saw fit to report what transpired. At one point Hooper also could have lived in Barnet as, when indicted for riotous behaviour and committing a breach of the peace at the Knowland–Walsh fight (see page 47), he was stated to be "late of the Parish of Chipping Barnet". It was possibly during this period that he and the artist George Morland chanced upon each other at Whetstone turnpike, a meeting described by the Scottish poet

Allan Cunningham when writing of the eminent 18th-century painter. Morland's antipathy towards the aristocracy and his propensity for mixing with low-class acquaintances is well documented. However, he was occasionally somewhat ashamed of his 'friendships' with the latter and, on this particular day, chose not to recognize the 'Tinman' who, accompanied by a chimney-sweep, was characteristically arguing with the toll-collector. Hooper, though, refused to be ignored and was insistent that the reluctant Morland also acknowledged his companion. The incident is said to have greatly embarrassed the painter, who felt that the pugilist's conduct had demeaned him in the eyes of his fellow travellers.

It was Hooper's misfortune to be backed by the infamous Lord Richard Barrymore (known as 'Hellgate'), a depraved member of the aristocracy whom, it is believed, he first met at the Cotterell fight. He became Barrymore's personal retainer and, although he went on to beat such highly regarded men as Bob Watson, George Maddox and Bill Wood, he was drawn into his employer's dissolute lifestyle which ultimately destroyed his health. This "table-companion of peers" died in abject poverty at St Giles's Workhouse where he had been conveyed, emaciated and in rags, by a chimney-sweep who had found him expiring in the street. The date was either 27 or 28 April 1799, six years after the untimely demise of his notorious patron who accidentally shot himself in March 1793. Barrymore is thus exonerated of the accusation by Miles that he deserted his 'minder' and left him to perish in wretched circumstances. Indeed, at the time of Barrymore's death Hooper was still unbeaten and would remain so for a further three years.

The Times Condemns Proposed Match

The Times newspaper, on 22 September 1789, highlighted its prejudices against prize-fighting with adverse comments about a contest scheduled to be fought at Finchley:

> Notwithstanding all that has been said, a boxing match is this day to take place in the vicinity of London, between two of those noted blackguards who are eternally disturbing the peace of society. Surely, as the magistrates have had timely notice of this intended breach of the law, they will do their endeavours to interdict it. We cannot suppose them influenced to the contrary by any motives whatsoever, – Finchley is the place fixed for drawing the croud [*sic*], where many a spectator will be robbed before his return to town. All the pickpockets and sharpers in London have had timely notice to attend.

Unfortunately the paper did not follow up on the story so there is no way of knowing whether the magistrates heeded its fervent exhortations to prevent the bout or, indeed, who the participants might have been. The above is, however, an excellent example of *The Times'* highly critical attitude to the sport at the very period when the prize-ring enjoyed the patronage of some of the country's most influential figures. Some decades later the *Weekly Dispatch*, once an enthusiastic supporter of boxing, would adopt a similar attitude; by this time, though, pugilism had begun its long downward slide into ignominy and the *Dispatch's* viewpoint consequently had somewhat wider support.

Bruising Butchers

Throughout the history of prize-fighting the trade of butcher produced more first-rate bruisers than any other of the varied occupations from which the sport drew its ranks. Possibly the earliest reference to a pugilistic 'knight of the cleaver' can be found in the *True Protestant Mercury* of 31 December-4 January 1681-82. (Some sources place the January in 1681 rather than 1682 because with the old style Julian calendar, then still in operation, the new year began in March.) The newspaper recorded a "Match of Boxing" between an unnamed butcher and the Duke of Albermarle's footman, the former being declared "the best at that Exercise in England".

In the 18th century the tradition continued with men of the calibre of Jack Slack, Bill Purdue and Sam Martin, together with the spirited Bristol lightweight Bob Watson and Bill Ward's brother Joe. (*Boxiana* stated that the last-named was an engraver's apprentice, but contemporary newspapers generally referred to him as a butcher.) To this list could probably be added Tom Treadaway, although insufficient information precludes a fully accurate assessment of his ability. Certainly Egan believed his efforts were "entitled to respectable mention" whilst *The Star*, in recounting his only well-chronicled contest (against Joe Lashley), called him the "noted Tedaway". This description was also used by the *Sporting Magazine* when reporting Treadaway's later bout with a wheelwright by the name of Conway, although on that occasion his name was spelt correctly.

Treadaway is known to have appeared at least once in the Barnet area prior to his match with Lashley, whose victory in their contest on 13 June 1791 is thought to mark the first fistic success in England by a black fighter. The *Whitehall Evening-Post* of Thursday 24 to Saturday 26 September 1789 declared that a "long depending Battle" would be fought at Finchley on Tuesday of the following week between "one Treddaway [*sic*] of Oxford market" and Thomas Marshal of Carnaby Market, locally referred to as 'Long Tom'. The newspaper was anticipating a gruelling encounter as it stated that neither of the combatants had ever entered the prize-ring before. Apparently Hooper was to second Treadaway and Tom Tring his opponent. The *Oracle Bell's New World* of 29 September confirmed that two butchers would be meeting that day at Finchley in a confrontation which it expected to be "very hardily contested". Both journals, though, neglected to report the fight and, with no other sources now available to supply any details, the meagre information provided by Egan has to suffice. He was unable to furnish the date, length or, indeed, number of rounds fought but did write that the set-to occurred on Finchley Common for 20 guineas a side and that Treadaway was the winner. This last statement was borne out by *The Star*, which described Treadaway as "never before having been beat" in its account of the Lashley match. Egan also agreed that Marshal was a butcher so presumably Treadaway's ardent support from his fellow purveyors of meat, which was to be extremely conspicuous at the Lashley bout, must have been considerably reduced against 'Long Tom'.

"Rioters and Routers and Disturbers of the Peace"

A battle between Nowland the Irish Chairman, and Welch an Irish Taylor, was fought at Barnet on Monday last, which terminated in favour of the former. A violent affray took place in the road to town, between some of the Amateurs, which ended in broken heads and bloody noses.

The Star (Friday 12 October 1792) contained the above sparse account of an occasion not considered sufficiently newsworthy to be reported in any other surviving daily paper then showing an interest in pugilistic activity. The encounter itself was certainly of little significance, although it is probable that one of the boxers, Nowland, was the same man who had previously tested Bill Wood in a match that historians have omitted to include on the celebrated coachman's record. What made the Barnet affair somewhat unusual was the concerted resistance shown by the Fancy against an attempt by the Justices of the Peace and constables of the parish to curtail the contest. A fight crowd, although by nature unruly, usually acted with respect towards any officers of the law attempting to interrupt its entertainment. Indeed it was far from uncommon for just one magistrate or JP single-handedly to halt a bout attended by hundreds of men who, under other circumstances, often had scant regard for authority. However, the Liberty of St Albans Quarter Sessions Roll for 1793, recording the indictments of the three ringleaders who incited the violent opposition, makes it clear that, on this occasion at least, the spectators "obstinately, unlawfully and riotously" refused to disperse. The exact location of the clash is not given in this source, but the minute book for the relevant sessions states it to be "Barnett Comon [*sic*]".

The 'Tinman', Bill Hooper, was one of the men indicted. Accused at the same Epiphany Sessions, which commenced at St Albans on 17 January 1793, were John Butcher, a St Marylebone coachmaster, and William Jacklin, a Holborn labourer also known by the name of Johnson. The former was most likely the Jack Butcher who had been Hooper's bottle-holder against Cotterell, whilst the latter was undoubtedly Tom Johnson's brother, Bill Jackling. (The former champion of England, described in the sessions roll as being a victualler in Duke Street, Lincoln's Inn Fields, stood surety for his younger sibling.) Jackling himself was a competent bruiser and *The Star* had commented two years before, after his defeat of the 'Ruffian', John Symonds, that he fought with more courage, albeit less skill, than his famous brother.

Entries in the gaol book for the Liberty and the Borough of St Albans show that Butcher and Jackling were found guilty of "committing a Riot" and sentenced respectively to three and two months' incarceration in the prison located within the gateway of St Albans Abbey. They were also ordered to pay £100 each and to find a surety of the same sum, both amounts to be forfeited if they failed to keep the peace for a period of two years. In the case of Jackling this was later increased to three years at the following sessions. There was no mention of Hooper so it may be presumed that he was found not guilty. If so, this seems a rather strange decision since it is hard to believe that the belligerent 'Tinman' would have been any less involved in the affray than Butcher or Jackling. Perhaps Lord Barrymore brought his aristocratic, or more likely financial, influence to bear on behalf of his pugnacious retainer whilst Hooper's co-defendants, lacking such an affluent patron, were left to suffer the consequences of their "warlike" actions.

The combatants involved in the prize-fight itself were also indicted. Both men were stated in the sessions roll to be "late of Chipping Barnet" and the spelling of their names differed from the report in *The Star*. Patrick Knowland's occupation was given as labourer and Patrick Walsh's as tailor. A letter to the court from one Lewis Henry, of the parish of St George's, Hanover Square, apologized for not being able to appear personally on behalf of Walsh whom he had known for eight years and always found to be "an honest sober and well behaved man". Henry, a fellow tailor who may have been the protagonist's employer, also wrote that "it is the first time I ever new [*sic*] him to fight a Pitch [*sic*] Battle". This character endorsement seems to have had some influence on the court for Walsh received a less severe sentence than Butcher and Jackling despite being convicted on the same charge. He was in prison for just one week, ordered to pay the sum of £20 and fined a surety of £10 to keep the peace for one year (later increased to three years). Again there was a definite anomaly in that an entry for Knowland, surely just as guilty as Walsh, cannot be found in the gaol book.

PART II - THE MIDDLE YEARS

We now must sing of Belcher's fame,
Whose race was full of glory;
His matchless deeds I need not name,
You all must know his story.

Frederick Lawson

The Bristolian Belchers

The advent of the 19th century brought to the area Jem Belcher, grandson of Jack Slack and destined to become one of the prize-ring's greatest exponents. Belcher, another butcher, hailed from Bristol at the time when this West Country city was fast emerging as a hotbed of pugilistic talent. He was only 19 when he appeared in a bout with the 37-year-old Brentford-born Jack Bartholomew at Finchley Common. (According to the maps of John Cary, the premier cartographer of the age, the common around that time was approximately three miles long, one and a half miles wide and covered most of the area now occupied by both North and East Finchley.)

6. Jem Belcher, a grandson of Broughton's conqueror Jack Slack and one of the prize-ring's foremost exponents.

Belcher introduced an original style to the sport; little more than a middleweight, he found it expedient to utilize greater movement than was generally customary during this period. His knowledge of the art was largely intuitive, his agility little short of extraordinary and his 'bottom' undoubted. Belcher's adversary, a long-time favourite of the Fancy, was an extremely game battler and the possessor of considerable power. The combatants had previously met once before in a gruelling encounter which had eventually terminated in a draw. The rematch, on 15 May 1800, saw Bartholomew, the stronger and heavier of the two, attempt to maximize his physical attributes whilst Belcher wisely opted to mill on the retreat.

The veteran gained the first major advantage, felling the future champion in the second round with such a heavy punch that his chances of recovery seemed remote. In fact Bartholomew's supporters, prematurely deciding that victory was a foregone conclusion, sent a carrier pigeon to London with news of their man's success. However, the Bristolian showed the bravery and recuperative powers expected from a descendant of the celebrated Slack. A few minutes later he completely turned the contest around with a well executed cross-buttock throw. The *Oracle, and the Daily Advertiser* of the following day reported that Bartholomew "was thrown upon his head with such violence that his eye-sight failed him and he appeared infinitely distressed". From then on he was never quite able to provide the same formidable resistance but still continued courageously to dispute every round until, at length, he received a tremendous blow to the pit of the stomach which ended the proceedings. Although the battle lasted only 20 minutes, as the *Sporting Magazine* commented, it was "seventeen rounds of as severe fighting as we ever remembered".

Immediately afterwards the loser was taken into custody by police officers under the authority of a judge's warrant and was escorted back to town, where he was bailed on arrival. The next week the *Morning Post and Gazetteer* explained that he had been arrested "for having forfeited his bond to keep the peace given at the time he was tried for killing a man at Charing Cross". (This probably referred to an affray in which a sailor, James Hayes, met his death at the hands of John Symonds on 30 January 1798 at the Crown and Thistle public house. Bartholomew was subsequently tried for aiding and abetting his fellow bruiser in the slaying of the unfortunate seaman.) After succumbing to the youthful Belcher, Bartholomew never fought again and the *Sporting Magazine* recorded his demise in

7. Jack Bartholomew, a respected veteran by the time he fought Jem Belcher at Finchley.

July 1803, in the Almonry, Westminster, after an illness of several months. Following a death-bed request, his body was opened and it was found that his liver was "remarkably enlarged and quite scirrhous".

Belcher's impressive performance at Finchley confirmed his position as a genuine title claimant. In his very next bout he easily overcame unbeaten Irishman Andrew Gamble to earn recognition as champion of England. He went on to quell the powerful Shropshire brawler Joe Bourke (Berks) four times, twice in turn-ups, and also scored a 20-minute victory over Jack Firby before losing an eye in an unfortunate rackets accident. This led to his early retirement, but he was injudiciously tempted back into the ring with his former protégé Henry Pearce and later, on two occasions, against the redoubtable Tom Cribb. In all three meetings Belcher found his restricted vision to be too great a handicap and was reluctantly forced to admit defeat. He passed away at the early age of thirty, on 30 July 1811, leaving behind a well-deserved reputation as the most brilliant pugilist of his day. An interesting footnote to Jem's story is that he made popular the wearing of colours by fighters and gave his name to the neckerchief, known as the 'Belcher', which later became an item of high fashion.

8. Tom Belcher, the younger brother of the celebrated Jem and himself an extremely skilful pugilist.

Another of the Belcher clan, younger brother Tom, although not quite reaching the heights of his famous elder sibling, was nevertheless a noted performer known for his skill and sparring abilities. He had a distinguished career in which he clashed three times with the renowned 'Dutch Sam', and twice beat that determined Irish hero Dan Dogherty, one of the latter matches being made by Lord Byron. In 1814 he took over the running of the Castle Tavern in Holborn, for many years the unofficial headquarters of the ring. Tom was one of the 18 boxers employed at the crowning of George IV and the lucky recipient of the single gold coronation medal presented to this corps of royal pages to commemorate the momentous event.

In 1828 he retired as landlord of the Castle Tavern and took up residence in Finchley. Egan related in *Boxiana* that "the lucky Tom Belcher now passes his days in a very handsome cottage on Finchley Common, living at his ease like a man of fortune, with his dog and his gun, to traverse the fields when he feels inclined for a day's shooting to 'bag the game'". Belcher later moved from the area and his death certificate recorded that he died from apoplexy at his house in Trafalgar-square, Park Road, Peckham, on 9 December 1854.

Pig Displays the White Feather

Ikey Pig was a ponderous Jewish bruiser whose sole claim to fame was that he once shared a ring with the future champion, Tom Cribb. Since he was of Hebrew origin it is extremely improbable that Pig was his real name. More likely, as suggested in an article on Jewish pugilists which appeared in the *St. James's Gazette* of 17 August 1886, his surname was Pick. The match with Cribb, which took place at Blackheath in May 1805, lasted some 25 minutes before Pig, claiming a sprained wrist, retired prematurely. Much the stronger man, his supporters had introduced him to the fistic world as the "Jewish Ajax" and the manner of his defeat caused them considerable distress. The contest is generally listed as being his only regular prize-ring appearance, but in fact he took part in another bout the following year in which he was apparently once more guilty of showing the white feather.

The confrontation between Pig and Isaac Wood, a waterman, was one of three pitched battles arranged for Thursday 3 July 1806 at Wood Green. No sooner had these second-rate boxers begun their preparations, however, than they were unceremoniously disturbed by a "formidable party of Police Officers". Two days later *The Times* described how, after several vehicles had been overturned, the motley assemblage decided to proceed to Finchley. There they had great expectations of an uninterrupted encounter but hopes were swiftly dashed when the forces of law and order again appeared on the scene. Opportunities for holding the fight elsewhere were non-existent due to the diligent attentions of the officers, who stuck closely to the rabble as they took a circuitous route back to town. Unable to lose their determined pursuers, the mob finally admitted defeat and the affair had to be left temporarily undecided.

On the following Monday a disreputable crowd gathered on Highgate Common for the ostensible purpose of a bull-bait. However, as *The Sun* eloquently reported, "the real object of the meeting was to decide an adjourned contest between two animals of the same blood, but without the same quantity of either legs or horns". The diversion of bull-baiting had its desired effect for, on this occasion, Pig and Wood were able to resolve their differences without molestation. The former had the advantage of strength; in the early rounds he was generally able to make the first hit and prevail in the short rallies which followed. The exchanges became more prolonged and equal as the contest progressed and both men suffered disfiguration about the head. After 40 minutes Pig fell, and no amount of effort on the part of his frantic seconds could induce him to the scratch in time. The loser was greatly derided and *The Courier* contemptuously remarked that he should give up all pretensions of being a pugilist after such an ignominious defeat by a man "so much inferior in all the requisites of bruising".

Mayor Voids Contest

Charles Brannam, a carpenter's apprentice from Westminster, was barely 14 when he began his pugilistic career in December 1804. By the time he met a brickmaker called Brooks at Barnet, on 4 October 1808, he had amassed experience well beyond his tender years. Brooks was backed, for ten guineas, by Jem Belcher, who had been unsuccessful the year before when matching George Humphries against Brannam. The bout was originally scheduled for Finchley Common, but the unwelcome arrival of some peace officers resulted in an enforced move northwards. On reaching Barnet Common, a ring was swiftly established and the combatants set to, only to be halted after 35 minutes of hard-fought action by the mayor himself, accompanied by several constables. The outcome of the encounter was therefore left in doubt.

Brannam's career seems to have ended in disgrace only 18 months later. *Pancratia* described how, on 12 April 1810, he was involved in a "sham fight" with Charles Dixon in front of a large gathering of the Fancy. Pre-contest rumours that the protagonists intended to put on a bloodless display and afterwards share the reward were soon confirmed. Following half an hour of evasive milling Brannam gave in but "much to their disappointment, not a farthing was allowed them, and they sneakingly sheered off, dreading the indignation of the mob".

Kite Grounded by Drover

An interesting little battle was fought on 12 July 1810 between a drover by the name of Dawson and one Kite, described by *The Star* as "a second-rate fighting man". The mill, on Finchley Common for a sum of £5, was to settle a quarrel which had originated when Kite drank the drover's beer at a public house in Camden Town and then proceeded to kick him for having the audacity to grumble.

During the first six rounds of the 30-minute contest Dawson was on the receiving end, but thereafter he seized the initiative. *Bell's Weekly Messenger* of 15 July reported that "by going in and hitting, his strength and game baffled science and he paid his adversary in his own coin to the satisfaction of a numerous ring".

Pugnacious Postboys

A snippet in the *Barnet Gazette* (13 March 1858) highlighted the increased revenue a prominent posting house, in this case the Green Man at Barnet, could obtain in the event of a major prize-fight. The example given was the second meeting between John Gully and Bob Gregson which took place at Sir John Sebright's park near Flamstead in Hertfordshire on 10 May 1808. The amounts received between 9 and 11 May, a record for the Green Man, were listed as follows:

For posting (187 pairs) ...	141	17	10 ¹/₂
Bills in the house ...	54	19	0
Baits in the yard ...	14	10	0
	211	6	10 ¹/₂

Post horse duty for the 3 days £23 3 6.

Posthouses were inns where horses were kept for the use of travellers and it was not unusual for the postboys employed there to exhibit a certain amount of milling ability. (If Humphries' 'Annals of Pugilism' can be relied upon, the earliest example of a fighting postboy at Barnet was in the battle in August 1776, in which Bristolian Peter Bath overcame William Allen, the Clare Market butcher.)

The competition between rival posting establishments, particularly during the heyday of the coaching age, was bitter and intense. Nowhere was this more apparent than in Barnet. The Green Man, used as a posthouse by Lord Melbourne and other prominent Whigs, was in opposition to the Red Lion which was especially favoured by members of the Tory Party. The feud between the hostelries led to a legal wrangle involving Mr Thomas Newman, postmaster of the Green Man, and his counterpart at the Red Lion, Mr Charles Bryant. Employees of the two innkeepers also found themselves in court as the enmity increased. Amongst these was a notorious local character by the name of Richard Crouch, described by *Kent's Weekly Dispatch and Sporting Mercury* as "a celebrated pugilist".

Crouch, who at the time was working at the Green Man, appeared in a crowded session-house in St Albans, on Monday 19 July 1819, accused of assaulting two servants belonging to Mr Bryant. The incident followed a dispute over the supplying of four posthorses to Sir Robert Peel, the future prime minister. Crouch, stated the *Globe and Traveller* of 23rd July, had a fearsome reputation as the "terror of the neighbourhood" and was therefore a useful man for Mr Newman to have in his service. However, his fighting prowess, and that of his colleagues, failed to prevent the opposition succeeding in the honour of posting Sir Robert, a defeat which severely rankled with the pugnacious bully. He afterwards extracted a painful revenge on two members of the victorious team. William Cross was ruthlessly beaten until he managed to flee, whilst Edward Simpson was hammered into unconsciousness by the heavy fists of his assailant.

For the defence, it was argued that an over-zealous approach to the situation had possibly resulted in improper violence by both parties. The point was also made that, since the prosecutors had managed to secure Sir Robert's business, they were being somewhat churlish in bringing about the indictments. Witnesses were then called who stated that there had been provocation on both sides. The assaults not being denied, though, Crouch was found guilty and sentenced to pay a £30 fine for each charge, in addition to being confined for two months in the prison at St Albans. An individual called John Pratt, also in the service of Mr Newman, was incarcerated for one month and fined £10 for attacking another Red Lion employee, William Seymour. The lenient sentences, certainly in comparison with those given out for very minor offences involving personal possessions, reflected the strong bias the legal system of the period had in favour of property, and its corresponding lack of concern regarding any violence on persons which stopped short of murder.

Five days later Thomas Newman himself appeared at the Court of Chancery, Lincoln's Inn, in a case which apparently "gave rise to considerable mirth". (The Chancery court administered the rules of equity rather than common law. Although it was meant to dispense 'natural justice', it ironically became more corrupt than the conventional courts, being synonymous with excessive fees and bribery.)

The motion was made that Mr Newman should be committed to Fleet Prison for blatantly disregarding an order served on him not to interfere with his rival's posting trade. The counsel for the plaintiff, according to both the *Globe* and the *Public Ledger, and Daily Advertiser* of 26 July, detailed various circumstances relating to the defendant's obstruction of Mr Bryant's business, in particular the engaging of "prizefighters to prevent his post-boys from approaching the chaises which drove up to the Red Lion". (For some reason, later books describing the feud attribute the gang of bruisers to Mr Bryant but the Liberty of St Albans court records and contemporary newspapers leave no doubt that they are in error.) Mr Newman's counsel denied all allegations and argued that the pugilists said to be working for the defendant were, in reality, nothing more than general employees. The decision of the court was that the offence was not serious enough to warrant imprisonment; Mr Newman was ordered to pay the costs, but this curious little saga was not yet completely at an end.

Both Crouch and Pratt languished in prison for longer than their allotted sentences. The gaol book for the Liberty of St Albans Quarter Sessions has a last entry for Pratt of Easter 1820, and for Crouch of Midsummer 1821. Crouch's extended stay came about partly because, on the afternoon of 18 October 1819, he had escaped from a locked room at the head of the stairs on the second floor of the prison. This he had accomplished by inserting the end of a large faggot stick into the space between the staple and the bolt of the door lock. His task was made considerably easier by the fact that the gaoler had been remiss in not securing a second bolt and had also failed to fasten two further doors on the staircase. Crouch does not appear to have remained free for very long, since a report in the 1820 Quarter Sessions roll states that, by 13 January, he had been reapprehended.

The 'Gasman' Extinguished

On 10 December 1822, a dreadful accident on Finchley Common took the life of Tom Hickman, whose battle with Bill Neat had been the subject of William Hazlitt's famous essay, 'The Fight'. Hickman, known as the 'Gasman', never attained the mantle of champion but, for a time, was considered virtually unbeatable by the Fancy. His loss to Neat, however, had such a devastating effect on him that he retired from the ring completely, although it is probable that he would have embarked on a come-back had not the disaster arisen.

Born in Dudley, Hickman showed natural fighting ability from an early age, both in his home town and subsequently on his arrival in the metropolis. His milling qualities having impressed the noted Tom Shelton, he was matched with Peter Crawley in March 1819. Despite sustaining a broken finger, Hickman scored an easy victory over the future champion. Two successful bouts with the scientific George Cooper and a win against the experienced Tom Oliver set up the Neat fight in which Hickman's aura of invincibility was irrevocably shattered.

On the day of the fatal accident, Hickman had travelled to Harpenden Common to watch the bout between Shelton, the man influential in his early career, and Josh Hudson who was being mooted as a possible future opponent. After witnessing Shelton's victory the 'Gasman' set out on his return journey to London. He was, in fact, singularly unsuited to be in charge of a vehicle, and the *Annals of Sporting and Fancy Gazette* even went as far as to say that "never was seen a worse driver, perhaps, than Tom Hickman". The evening was foggy and this may have been the reason why he attempted to overtake a wagon on the nearside of the road about half a mile north of the Green Man on Finchley Common. In doing so, he mounted a bank, overturned his chaise and precipitated himself and his passenger under the wheels of a

9. The unfortunate 'Gasman', Tom Hickman, whose untimely death occurred as the result of an accident on Finchley Common.

heavily laden cart being drawn by the wagon. Hickman was killed instantly and his companion, Thomas Rowe, a silversmith and jeweller from Aldersgate Street, survived only minutes longer. The mutilated bodies were conveyed to the Swan with Two Necks on the common where the sight of them reputedly so upset the landlord that he too expired within the week.

At the same public house the next evening an inquest was held before the coroner for Middlesex, Mr Thomas Stirling, and a large crowd from the sporting fraternity. Evidence was given by Chancy Barber, a Finchley bricklayer, and James Ball, a servant from Whetstone, which proved conclusively that the wagoner was in no way to blame for the tragic occurrence. A verdict of accidental death was therefore returned by the jury. Hickman was interred eight days later in a grave which *Bell's Life in London* described as more than 15 feet deep, the object being to thwart resurrectionists thought to be interested in stealing his body.

The *Annals of Sporting* felt that Hickman's violent demise was justice from providence for a supposed crime for which he had escaped legal punishment earlier the same year (although in fact it was actually the previous one). He was generally considered to have been responsible for the death of Joe Norton, the respected master of ceremonies at that showplace of sparring, the Fives Court. In a fit of temper he had attacked the much older man, who later complained of his injuries and died not long afterwards. Although the inquest on Norton attached no blame to Hickman, on the grounds that it could not be proved that the assault had occasioned the former's death, the 'Gasman' was believed to be accountable.

In addition to his appearance in Hazlitt's essay, Hickman also featured in a short story, originally published in the *Strand Magazine* of November 1921, written by the creator of Sherlock Holmes, Sir Arthur Conan Doyle. A boxing enthusiast, Conan Doyle's knowledge of the prize-ring was skilfully reflected in his various fictional tales of the sport. 'The Bully of Brocas Court' told of the fearsome ghost of Hickman appearing "between Finchley and Elstree" and challenging "passers-by to fight in the old style". The apparition of the pugilist, his head horribly mutilated, was attended by the ghost of Thomas Rowe.

Justifiable Homicide?

The Barnet area's first known prize-ring fatality happened on Saturday 9 July 1825 as a result of a quarrel at the Five Bells public house, East End Road, Finchley. John Platt, having lost a game of nine-pins to his fellow workman Thomas Jordan, refused to pay the resulting debt and thereafter became very abusive. Platt's behaviour and challenges to fight were initially ignored by the quiet and inoffensive Jordan. Eventually, however, when struck, his patience wore thin and he was further provoked by foul insults made to his wife. Following the landlord's warning that he would not allow them to settle their differences on his premises, the two adjourned to a nearby field and, with relatives as seconds, prepared to do battle. Platt was by far the bigger man and reputedly the better pugilist but his opponent had right on his side. Despite absorbing some severe blows and being thrown heavily several times, Jordan managed to survive and, at length, terminated the conflict by felling his adversary with a violent punch to the abdomen. Platt was carried from the field and, though later attended by a surgeon, died in great pain the next day.

An inquest took place on the Tuesday at the Red Lion on nearby Red Lion Hill before Thomas Stirling, the same coroner who had presided over the Hickman post-mortem some two and a half years earlier. He expressed the opinion that no man could be expected to endure excessive violence and abuse, especially in front of his wife, without giving in to provocation and resorting to fisticuffs. One of the jurors, obviously strongly opposed to prize-fighting, believed the public ought not to be exposed to these illegal acts and that therefore, however extenuating the circumstances, Jordan should not escape punishment. His view that men ought to be put in a cage when such situations arose on a publican's property earned a retort from the coroner that he would then hate to be a landlord "as he should expect to have his head knocked about a good many times". Other jurors concurred with Mr Stirling's earlier sentiments. Whilst keen to put a stop to milling, they were in agreement that this was not an instance where the accused could be blamed. Even so, they were not inclined to return a verdict of justifiable homicide, so instead recorded that "the deceased died of an inflammation in the bowels, in consequence of the blows he received in a fight with Thomas Jordan, who gave them in his own defence".

Although papers such as *Bell's Life in London*, the *Weekly Dispatch* and *Bell's Weekly Messenger* all reported similar details, *The Times* carried a completely different story. Its version of events had John Platt arguing with one Leonard at the Red Lion on the Saturday night about the prowess of each man and, rather than the other's wife being involved, there was a mention of a "female of Leonard's acquaintance". Furthermore this account related that the confrontation did not take place until Monday 11 July, with the defeated man dying a few minutes after receiving the fatal blow.

'Young Gas' Resists Temptation

The events of October 1825 leading up to the non-appearance of Reuben Marten for a contest with 'Young Gas' were indicative of the dishonesty creeping back into boxing at a level not seen since the days prior to Tom Johnson. Pierce Egan and George Kent had both warned their readers the previous year of declining standards within the prize-ring, and the demise, the month after the Marten fiasco, of the respected Pugilistic Club, an administrative institution dedicated to fair play, only served to emphasize the problems facing the sport.

'Young Gas' (as Jonathan Bissel was known) bore a strong resemblance to the original 'Gasman', Tom Hickman, both in appearance and style of fighting, although he could not be considered to be of the same calibre. It was during his training at Whetstone that he had his first experience of the chicanery that was to surround the planned Marten bout. He was approached by one James Smith, a muffin baker from Gray's Inn Lane, who promised him £200, a substantial amount at the time, if he would consent to throw the contest. The proposition was repeated on two further occasions but, the *Morning Herald* was delighted to note, "Young Gas was too honest to sell the national character for such a trifle". The attempted bribery and later duplicity involved were a good example of the spreading corruption but at least Gas's probity in resisting temptation showed there was some honour left to combat the increasing degeneration.

Despite his refusal to be bribed, Bissel nevertheless believed the encounter would still take place. His optimism seemed justified when, two days before the date appointed for the mill, he received a visit from Marten at which it was agreed that the latter would accept 50 shillings in order that Gas's nomination of the place of battle be adopted. However, as *Bell's Life in London* pointed out, "Marten must have very well known, at that time, that his friends did not intend him to fight at all". The purpose of his trip to Whetstone could only have been to maintain the delusion of normality (in addition, of course, to obtaining an acceptable little windfall).

The venue that 'Young Gas' had selected was Harpenden, and on 18 October he made his way to St Albans, where he learned that Marten had managed to get himself bound over to keep the peace in the county of Hertfordshire. For this convenient situation the reluctant bruiser was indebted to his dutiful wife, who had informed the 'beaks' that her husband was to participate in the impending match. To ensure that Marten did not use the interference of the law as a reason for his failure to set to with Bissel, the location was switched to just within the confines of Bedfordshire. Predictably, Marten made the decision not to appear and 'Gas', having thrown his hat into the ring in the customary fashion, entered the roped area to lay claim to the stake money.

It was left to 'Young Dutch Sam' (Samuel Evans), generally supposed to be the son of the legendary Jewish pugilist 'Dutch Sam' and himself no mean performer, to provide the main entertainment by defeating the 'Sailor Boy', Harry Jones, in a bout thought to be somewhat suspect. The cabriolet driver Ned Savage, whose best and worst character traits will be highlighted shortly, then unsuccessfully clashed with hackney-coachman Jem Kirkman in the first of four meetings between these bitter rivals. Savage was later seen at Barnet where he seemed to be in a state of great suffering, although the 'hugging' nature of his contest could hardly have been responsible for reducing him to this condition. Reuben Marten too was espied in the town and "openly charged with making the match purposely for a cross", an accusation which he found difficult to refute.

On the following Wednesday a large gathering of the Fancy assembled at the Castle Tavern to arbitrate on a dispute regarding the stake money rightly due to 'Gas'. The 'plaintiff' again repeated his disclosure of attempted bribery, which he had originally made at ringside, but now cited Smith as being the man who approached him, probably on behalf of two other parties named Abbott and Priestley. The muffin baker was duly summoned, but refused to incriminate himself or his associates and there the matter had to rest. 'Gas' received £40 from the stakeholder, Tom Belcher, but it was not until April of the next year that he finally obtained the remaining £60 to which he was entitled (the contest having been made for £50 a side). He was subsequently beaten by Marten when the two did eventually face each other in October 1827.

A Convenient Stopping-place

10. The accomplished lightweight Barney Aaron, a particular favourite of the Jewish fistic fraternity.

About four miles from St Albans, and famous as the spot where the notorious 17th-century highwaywoman, Lady Katherine Ferrers, had been fatally wounded, No Mans Land was a popular locality for boxing encounters. The town of Barnet, due to its advantageous position, was much favoured by the London Fancy as a convenient stopping-place when contests were held at that venue.

Around the time Barney Aaron and Dick Hares (Ayres) were matched in spring 1826, No Mans Land was, in the opinion of the *Morning Chronicle*, one of the country's premier fistic locations, mainly because of the liberal attitude which the magistrates in the vicinity took to the sport. The bout, arranged for Tuesday 21 March, aroused a great deal of interest, particularly amongst those pugilistically inclined members of the Jewish community who could always be relied upon to muster strongly on behalf of Aaron. On arrival at Barnet, word was given that the encounter would take place at Colney Heath, rather than No Mans Land as had previously been determined. Aaron and his friends therefore made their way to the new battleground only to find it deserted. Deciding to repair to the village of Colney, they came across Hares and his supporters. Whilst the two groups were debating their next move, a messenger arrived with the information that the ring had been formed, after all, on the spot originally intended.

The mill proved to be a rather one-sided affair with the veteran Hares, despite valuable experience gained from a long career, struggling to cope with the science and youth of his accomplished opponent. In the 41st round a great commotion arose when Dick's second Peter Crawley, together with a vociferous body of Hares's friends, asserted that their man had received a foul blow. Aaron's party, including Crawley's counterpart Josh Hudson, was equally adamant that no such infringement had taken place. The two umpires disagreeing on the validity of Hares's claim, an appeal was made to the referee but he was unable to arbitrate as he had been unsighted when the incident occurred. More dissention inevitably followed on Hares's behalf, but by the time the referee had stated that whoever left the ring without fighting should be adjudged the loser, the ropes had been dismantled and some of the stakes pulled up. At this point Aaron remained within the stipulated area, ready to continue, whilst his adversary had been removed to a position further afield.

The ground being in a state of uproar and confusion, it was impossible for the umpires and referee to weigh up the merits of the case fully and they agreed to convene at a suitable spot on the way home to continue their discussions. A meeting at Barnet was decided upon and the attendance of both factions requested. Hares, however, along with his seconds and backer, was totally convinced that victory was his and proceeded through the town without deigning to stop. A little after six o'clock, in a private room at the

Green Man, the umpires and referee after some deliberation committed their version of events to paper. The umpire for Hares recorded that Dick had received a punch when on the ground, albeit an accidental one, and was therefore entitled to the stakes. Aaron's official wrote that he had witnessed the whole of the disputed round and at no time had he seen a foul blow being struck. It was the all-important opinion of the referee that the Jewish fighter should be given the battle money since Hares had declined to proceed with the bout when requested to do so.

Two days later, a meeting of the interested parties took place at the *Bell's Life in London* office. There the stakeholder informed the assembled company that he was compelled to act according to the referee's judgment. One of Hares's backers objected and threatened litigation, but an attorney's clerk who was present pointed out that such a course would serve no purpose as all pugilistic matters were considered to be of an illegal nature. The money, amounting to 50 sovereigns, was then handed over to Aaron. If it appears that more significance was attached to the final outcome than was perhaps warranted, it is worth bearing in mind that payment of many large bets depended on the stakeholder's action.

Savage Mêlée in the Mire

Originally planned for the neighbourhood of Hendon, the first contest between Ned Savage and Jem Wallace, on 6 March 1827, was prevented by a magistrate who refused to permit an affray in the area under his jurisdiction. The venue problem was resolved by a farmer offering the use of his property "through which the river Brent ran, dividing the two counties, of Middlesex and Hertford, in the latter of which the sports of the day might take place without the chance of interference". The decision was therefore taken to move on to Whetstone and the Swan with Two Necks became the agreed rendezvous. However, while attempting to reach the appointed field, many of the scrambling throng fell into the river which had swelled as a result of a vicious rainstorm. Notwithstanding the difficulties experienced, after a temporary bridge of planks was constructed, an immense crowd of spectators had gathered by the time the fighters came to the scratch.

Savage had the advantage in weight, being 11 stone 6 pounds to his antagonist's 10 stone 8 pounds. He was seconded by Tom Gaynor and Peter Crawley, the latter having recently retired just a couple of days after his championship win over Jem Ward. Wallace, the more skilful of the two, had the support of Ben Burn, together with Jack Randall whose fistic achievements some years earlier had earned him the title of the 'Nonpareil'. During the bout continuous rain soaked the spectators and soon turned the ground into a mire. The two combatants, covered in mud, waged an even, determined battle for two hours, although action then understandably flagged. At length, after a marathon 127 rounds lasting 147 minutes, Wallace was so completely exhausted that his friends gave in for him.

Both men, totally insensible, were conveyed to the Swan, put to bed and bled. (This practice was then customary amongst the medical profession, but how it could help revive a fighter who had often already lost a lot of blood is difficult to comprehend – in fact, sometimes it could only have made matters worse.) The victor was in a much more serious condition than his opponent, and the *Weekly Dispatch* remarked that "fears for his life were at one time entertained by the surgeon who attended him". However, despite rumours of his demise on 8 March, a mere 24 hours afterwards Savage had recovered sufficiently to return to London. Less than three months later the pair again renewed their hostilities and on this occasion, at Banstead Downs, Wallace's improved science enabled him to turn the tables.

When the muddy mill was over, a new ring had to be formed in an adjoining field for the encounter between Isaac Dobell and Stephen Bailey. Although the stakes were for £50 a side, they fought more as a matter of honour than for financial gain since there was a history of bad feeling between the two. Dobell, the 28-year-old landlord of the Black Bull in Smithfield, was a powerfully built man; indeed *Pierce Egan's Weekly Courier* later stated that "his strength is so prodigious that he can lift from the ground eleven hundredweight". His opponent was a pork butcher, about 12 years older than Dobell, who worked in premises close to those of his adversary. Prior to the bout Bailey had trained at Barnet in an attempt to regain the condition he had enjoyed as a younger man in the Bristol prize-ring. However, the 37-minute contest, which did not commence until about six o'clock, ended in a victory for the publican after 38 spirited rounds.

Dobell scored a further success against Bailey the following year before twice capitulating to the well-regarded Tom Brown of Bridgnorth in 1829. Dobell was an interesting character inasmuch as he was ashamed of his pugilistic associations and eschewed the lifestyle of a prize-fighter, insisting instead that he be regarded purely as a tradesman.

Belcher's Novel Punchbag

Until the 19th century Kitts End, near Barnet, was a flourishing hamlet but two factors contrived to bring about its decline. One was the local Byng family's policy of increasing its Wrotham Park estate by buying up adjacent properties, and the other was the building of Thomas Telford's new road to St Albans in 1826, which diverted traffic and trade away from the area.

'Little Tim's Crib', described as being by the twelfth milestone at Kitts End, was known to be a popular training headquarters for fighters looking for suitable surroundings in which to prepare for their arduous ordeal ahead. The premises were almost certainly the Angel Inn, earlier the Crown, which was situated on the west side of Kitts End Road. This supposition is backed up by the fact that 'Little Tim's' was reported to have been run by one Timothy Davis, who was also listed in the Licensed Victuallers' Returns from 1808 to 1829 and in the South Mimms parish rate book for 1827 as being the licensee of the Angel. In addition, *Pigot and Co.'s London & Provincial New Commercial Directory, For 1823-4*, under the section "South Mimms", has the following entry: "Davis Timothy, Angel Public House".

The peaceful environment and welcoming hospitality at 'Little Tim's' must have played a big part in influencing Tom Belcher to take his charge Jem Burn to Kitts End during the month of March 1827. Burn, who had married Belcher's niece a year previously, came from good fighting stock and, at the start of his career, had been looked upon as a possible championship contender. However, losses to Ned Neale and Phil Sampson had reduced expectations by the time he stayed at Davis's crib prior to his bout with Ned Baldwin, popularly known as 'Whiteheaded Bob'. Part of Burn's exercise programme, devised by his famous mentor, involved his working two or three times a day with a well-stuffed haybag as a mock opponent – this was unusual in an age when training consisted primarily of long walks interspersed with occasional sparring. The regime obviously suited Burn for he defeated his favoured adversary in 33 minutes at No Mans Land on 24 April 1827.

The two boxers were matched for a second time on 3 July and again Burn trained at 'Little Tim's'. He was once more looked after by Tom Belcher, assisted by Jem's own uncle, Ben Burn, and Harry Harmer, another uncle of his wife. *Bell's Life in London* of 20 May mentioned that "Burn is about to commence the hay-sack gymnastics", and Egan commented in *Boxiana* that he had paid the greatest attention to the task in hand. Nevertheless, on this occasion, Belcher's novel punchbag failed in its purpose as Baldwin triumphed at Ruscombe Lake in Berkshire, after an exacting battle of one and a half hours.

Burn's second encounter with Baldwin was his penultimate ring appearance and he retired, following a further loss to Ned Neale, four months later. He subsequently became the landlord of two popular sporting hostelries in the West End of London, namely the Queen's Head Court in Windmill Street and the Rising Sun, Air Street. Despite retaining strong pugilistic links, Jem's competitive athletic days were thought to be well behind him when, in May 1842, he backed himself for £50 to walk ten miles in two and a half hours. The aristocratic gentleman who bet against him, after a difference of opinion regarding Burn's pedestrian abilities, was confident that the ex-boxer's bulk and "convivial propensities" made such an undertaking extremely unlikely. However, Burn demonstrated his determination by temporarily abandoning his thriving business to go into close training in Finchley, at the Five Bells. The result was that he shed a considerable amount of superfluous flesh, although on the day he was still believed to weigh somewhere in the region of 17 stone.

The "match against time" was scheduled for the end of May and *Bell's Life* (28 May) carried this brief notification: "29. Jem Burn to walk 10 miles in 2 1/2 hours, £50 a side, at the Five Bells, Finchley". A large number of Corinthians were drawn to the public house to witness the event and many heavy bets depended on the outcome. Burn began his attempt at five o'clock in the afternoon, after a one-mile course had been marked out and time-keepers appointed. Having managed four miles in 54 minutes, he stopped to refresh himself with sundry glasses of wine before going on to complete the full ten miles in 2 hours 16 minutes.

'Jack of Finchley'

The Barnet area produced a surprising paucity of documented prize-fighters, and in the 19th century none that could be considered of the first rank. Certainly John Brunston never aspired to major fistic heights, although he was described by *Bell's Life in London* as "a distinguished commoner, who had lowered the pride of all the navigators, brick makers, and macadamizers, in the rural vicinage of Finchley".

The only recorded contest for Brunston (commonly known as 'Jack of Finchley') took place at Colney Heath on 28 August 1827 after the third Ned Savage–Jem Kirkman encounter. The fight, for a collected purse of £2 (30 shillings to the winner and 10 to the loser), was against Bill Savage, believed at the time to be a far better boxer than his brother Ned. On setting to, Brunston immediately showed his gameness by stepping up to his opponent and punching away hard and fast to the head. Unhappily for the "countryman", however, his prowess did not quite match up to his courage and Savage was able to utilize his greater science to take command of the bout. Brunston showed good hitting ability but his adversary's straighter blows and tactical superiority ultimately enabled him to carry the day. The *Weekly Dispatch* asserted that the end came when the Finchley man gave in at the completion of the 20th round whilst *Bell's Life* maintained that Brunston had capitulated some six rounds earlier.

The two newspapers also disagreed on the role Jack's wife played in the day's proceedings. *Bell's Life* related how she tried in vain to persuade her husband to forgo the affair and then, having failed, began "piously praying that he might be 'well licked' for his pains". The *Weekly Dispatch's* version of the events was more colourful and it is not surprising therefore that the *Licensed Victuallers' Gazette* later preferred to base its account on this source. It considered that Brunston's wife had contributed to his defeat by insisting on remaining within the ropes where she continually harangued the unfortunate fighter. Apparently she "more than once made free use of her mauleys for the correcting those who dared to speak a word against her husband", all the while keeping up an incessant barrage of abuse regarding her opinion of his milling qualities. Indeed, according to the *Dispatch*, 'Jack of Finchley' blamed his wife for so intimidating him that he was unable to concentrate on the battle. Following the termination of the contest, the formidable Mrs Brunston led her conquered hero from the ring "promising to give him a rare time of it when she got him home".

A Little Set-to

On Wednesday 6 February 1828, a set-to occurred at Whetstone which was unusual, even by the broad-minded standards of the prize-ring, in that both protagonists were dwarfs. David Morgan, a 30-year-old Welshman trained by Ned Savage, stood 3 feet 9 inches tall, weighed less than 6 stone and was symmetrically proportioned. His opponent, 37-year-old Peter M'Bean from Perth, was 3 feet 6 inches in height; he had a large head and body, very short arms and, at 6 stone 7 pounds, enjoyed a not inconsiderable weight advantage. The unedifying spectacle took place in a 20-foot ring erected in a field close to the site of the Savage–Wallace fight. Despite the lack of interest shown by the Fancy, a large crowd was drawn to the event because of its strong novelty value.

Morgan worked steadily throughout whilst the Scotsman, since he was easily unbalanced, was forced to hold on to the ropes with one hand and attempt to hit with the other. These tactics being ineffective, M'Bean then resorted to butting and fared no better with this unsporting ploy; after 37 minutes his friends, seeing he had no chance, took him away. He was severely punished about the face whereas Morgan merely suffered a black eye and a damaged ear. The result was somewhat surprising as the loser had fought successfully at Newmarket, where he was a great favourite, and the winner was making his first pugilistic appearance.

After the main contest came a match which garnered little attention in the press at the time but was significant in that it marked the début of the renowned James Burke, popularly known as the 'Deaf'un'. Burke was born of Irish parents in December 1809, and in early life worked on the Thames waterfront. Here he was taken under

the wing of Joe Parish, a well-known former boxer, who was the landlord of a nearby public house. Both men were spectators at the Morgan–M'Bean encounter and, when ex-champion Peter Crawley collected a purse for a proposed second mill, Burke put himself forward as one of the combatants. Ned Murphy, a confident Irishman with previous ring experience, was the other volunteer.

Murphy wasted no time in attempting to dispatch his youthful opponent, but was met with telling counters. After some 20 rounds he realized the futility of charging his man and

11. James Burke, the game but eccentric 'Deaf'un'.

tried to draw Burke in, but the 'Deaf'un' would not be persuaded. Murphy himself then declined to become involved and, at the end of 50 rounds, when it was seen that the bout might continue indefinitely, the decision was taken to apportion the purse equally. Burke was disappointed with this stoppage, since he felt sure of victory, but expressed himself highly delighted with his share of the spoils. The 'Deaf'un' would subsequently fight at Whetstone on three more occasions as he took further steps on the road towards fistic honours. Murphy, in a letter in the *Weekly Dispatch* the following Sunday, blamed his poor performance on "drinking freely, being out late the night before, and walking down to Finchley on Wednesday morning". (This indicates that the contest took place on the 6th, as indeed the newspaper reported, rather than the generally accepted date of the 5th.)

The dwarfs were, for a short period of time, minor celebrities. As was usually the custom, a benefit was held for them and this attracted a good attendance. It took place at Isaac Dobell's Black Bull on 27 February, and in the sparring display which wound up the evening Morgan again had the upper hand, although M'Bean showed a significant improvement. Six days later the two were amongst the exhibitors at a benefit for Jack Carter, Lancashire's former self-proclaimed champion of England, who had recently been released from the convict hulks after serving a seemingly unjustified sentence for robbery. On this occasion *The Star* described their performance as affording "lots of fun".

Off-colour Brown Punished by Jewish Hero

Three weeks after the bizarre encounter involving Morgan and M'Bean, the same field was the scene of a meeting, for £5 a side, between Solomon Reubens and the 'Sprig of Myrtle', Ned Brown. The fight was originally fixed to take place in October 1827 but, the month before, the stakes on both sides had been withdrawn by mutual consent. Brown was well respected as a star of minor degree and had given the legendary lightweight Dick Curtis one of his severest battles. He had not fought since a fatal contest with the unfortunate Henry Scott in November 1824 (apart from an impromptu bout with the 'Colonel', Tom Reidie) and was consequently considered rather stale. Reubens was a rising favourite amongst the Jewish fraternity and had impressively beaten a Hoxton man by the name of Andrew Anderson just one month earlier. Two famous names acted in the capacity of seconds – Josh Hudson for Reubens could boast a win over champion Jem Ward, whilst Dick Curtis looked after his former adversary.

Prior to the start, several known pugilists forced back the unruly crowd in order to form an enclosure where spectators paying half a guinea could watch the proceedings in relative comfort. Amongst those performing this task were Jack Carter and Sam Tebbutts, now married to Tom Hickman's widow, Prudence. Since the match had been agreed only four days before and the training period therefore had been negligible, it was decided to increase the time allowed for coming up to the scratch to a full minute. The bout itself extended to 1 hour 45 minutes during which Brown absorbed terrible punishment whilst, in contrast, Reubens was hardly the worse for wear. The ring was repeatedly broken into but, as the *Morning Chronicle* recounted, "towards the conclusion Jack Carter came in like a second Goliah [*sic*], and with a large whip produced a quick retreat amongst the anxious throng". Thereafter the men were allowed to finish their labours uninterrupted. At length, in the 82nd round, the 'Sprig of Myrtle' was dropped in a helpless condition by a left to the mouth; when time was called, Curtis gave in for his man.

According to *Bell's Life in London* the numerous Jewish contingent, the like of which had not been seen at a mill since Barney Aaron's previous fight, "carried off their hero in triumph, and pulling up at Mr. Emms', The Crown, at Holloway, fought every round over again – historically, we mean – amidst oceans of brandy and water, and clouds from the odiferous weed".

Hasty Hostilities by the Roadside

Two minor bruisers, Jem Gray and Sam Hurn, had arranged to settle their differences for £5 a side on 14 April 1828 after a contest between Jem M'Carthy and Tom Ballard at Colney Heath. However, when both boxers happened to stop at the Green Man in Whetstone for refreshments on their way to the scene of action, their unplanned confrontation precipitated a premature set-to. It occurred despite fervent pleas for the fighters to control their contentious inclinations for a couple of hours in order not to jeopardise the day's sport.

All entreaties having been ignored, a makeshift ring was erected by the roadside in a field close to the public house and the eager antagonists immediately came to blows. Gray, far more experienced, dominated from the off and after the third round Hurn was a beaten man; only his bravery kept him going for another seven rounds until the contest was terminated in favour of his opponent. The bout, lasting 20 minutes, was considered to be one of the most one-sided ever witnessed in the area.

Mixed Fortunes for the Patlanders

The clash between Charley Jones, whose sparring abilities had earned him minor recognition, and the St Giles Irishman Ned Garvan came about on 8 May 1828 as a result of the latter's refusal, having lost at toss, to pay for a bottle of wine. Jones, so the *Weekly Dispatch* believed, resembled in size and mien the unbeaten 'Young Dutch Sam'. There, however, the similarity ended for his only previous experience of bareknuckle combat had been in one or two insignificant turn-ups. Garvan was also new to the prize-ring, although he had apparently acquitted himself well enough in several impromptu encounters around the vicinity of Primrose Hill.

The stakes having been pitched on a dry area of turf on Old Oak Common, Jones entered the ring and was preparing for action when two 'traps' from the Marlborough Street Office made an unexpected appearance. One of these unwelcome arrivals waved his baton in the face of Harry Jones, who was about to second his cousin, and demanded in the King's name that all parties present keep the peace. Since the officers' authority extended throughout the county of Middlesex, a hastily arranged council of war determined to proceed towards Hertfordshire, and hence a procession of horses and disgruntled pedestrians was soon on the move. A brief halt at the Welsh Harp found the forces of law and order still very much in attendance, so the long trek continued through Finchley and on to Whetstone. There, at the Swan with Two Necks, a local farmer was persuaded, for the sum of 30 shillings, to allow the use of one of his fields. This, *Bell's Life in London* described as being situated "at some distance from the road, in Hertfordshire, and divided from the forbidden ground by a small stream". The persistent 'traps' had followed their quarry to the village but, realizing that the battle would now take place out of their jurisdiction, retired to a neighbouring hostelry to enjoy some well-earned refreshment.

A second ring was quickly formed and, at a quarter to five, the protagonists made another appearance. Garvan sported a green handkerchief with yellow spots in deference to his Emerald Isle origins, and Jones a 'yellowman', traditionally the choice of Bristolian pugilists since it originated from Jem Belcher. (As referred to earlier, it was Belcher himself who popularized the wearing of colours. It became customary for the combatants' handkerchiefs, or 'fogles', to be entwined on one of the stakes, with the winner being entitled to claim possession of both as a trophy of victory. In 1838 this accepted practice became part of the 'New Rules'.)

When business finally commenced, the numerous lower-order patrons of milling no doubt wondered why they had endured such hardship to attend, for the engagement was an utterly dismal one throughout. The strong Irish contingent must have been particularly upset to discover that their man, in the words of the *Weekly Dispatch*, "was a mere old woman", and they would certainly have perceived his running tactics to be a severe affront to Hibernian manhood. Jones, as might be expected from one adept with the gloves, showed superior science and was also an accurate hitter, although his performance was more akin to that of a sparring bout than a regular contest. He nevertheless had the better of the few real exchanges and appeared to be heading for success when, in the 34th round, he threw a punch as his opponent fell. It was clear by now that being a recipient of a foul blow was the only method by which Garvan could legitimately triumph. His supporters vociferously clamoured for a favourable decision but, with no referee and the umpires divided on the issue, the dispute raged acrimoniously for some time.

At length Garvan's second, Paddy Flynn, brought his charge once more to the scratch and the fight was renewed, to the great disgust of the Irish mob who immediately began determined efforts to end the affair. The usual tactics were employed, with the ropes being cut and the ring invaded. Anyone who unwisely attempted to interfere was heavily beaten with sticks and forced to flee. The battles outside the ring provided the action that was lacking within, but this was of little consolation to Jones's friends and those present who were admirers of fair play. Surprisingly, given that Garvan had no chance of winning if the bout continued, his corner remonstrated with the troublemakers. Somehow, sufficient space was obtained for events to be brought to a conclusion, the St Giles fighter giving in after 53 rounds lasting one and a half hours.

The mill that followed was a far more manly one, and this time the Hibernian rabble had a hero of whom they could be justly proud. Dudley Downs was a young printer recently imported from Dublin where his fistic prowess had been thoroughly proven. Also a resident of the pugnacious settlement of St Giles, this was his first appearance in the London prize-ring and he seemed well equipped to restore the dented pride of his countrymen. He was opposed by a veteran in the shape of Ned Mason, a man known to have "fought many good battles in his better days" but who now plied his trade as a waiter in Reuben Marten's Soho establishment.

Downs soon took the lead and continued to demonstrate admirable coolness during the 33-minute encounter. He picked his shots with the maturity of a seasoned performer and did not allow a deep cut under his left eye to disturb his concentration. His adversary was obviously past his prime but still found the target with some savage body blows while uncomplainingly absorbing heavy punishment about the face. In the 12th round a flush hit on Mason's nose brought forth a stream of blood and, with a severely lacerated ear clearly evident, the waiter began to appear decidedly damaged. Three rounds later a right hand to the side of the head completely disorientated him, and when Marten and Charley Gybletts in Mason's corner were unable to bring their charge to the scratch in time, Downs was declared a popular winner. The Irishman's domination of the bout ensured that the crowd's behaviour was exemplary throughout and at its conclusion, as *The Star* reported, "the Patlanders shouted victory with a glee rendered doubly uproarious from their former defeat".

Bye-battles at Whetstone

Mike Murphy, younger brother of Ned, made the first of two appearances in the area when he fought George Bolton from Clare Market, for £10 a side, in a field near Whetstone. The tedious affair, on 29 July 1828, lasted one and a quarter hours and Murphy dominated from start to finish. By the conclusion Bolton showed considerable signs of damage but the victor escaped with only a slight injury to his lip.

The second bye-battle of the day involved James Burke who, following his début against the elder Murphy at Whetstone five months before, encountered one George Murray. This was much to the chagrin of Tom Hands who had seconded Bolton in the previous fight and was himself anxious to face the 'Deaf'un'. The contest was for a small purse and featured shrewd tactics from Burke to negate the fact that Murray was more than his equal in science. Every time the two men came to the scratch he rushed in and attempted to throw his opponent, thereby utilizing his superior strength whilst preventing Murray from displaying his boxing skills. At the end of 45 minutes the latter was forced to concede owing to a shoulder injury sustained when being thrown. As for Hands, yet another of the belligerent breed hailing from Clare Market, he received his chance not long afterwards but could do nothing to threaten Burke's blossoming reputation.

Cobbler Plucked by 'Gybletts' Chicken'

A large group from the East End of London descended on Whetstone on Monday 29 September 1828 to see two of their own do battle for £10 a side. Postponed from the previous Thursday, the fight did not attract many of the seasoned ring-goers since both men were largely unknown to the Fancy. The occasion was the début of Bill Fitzmaurice, a shipwright residing in Ratcliffe Highway and a pupil of Charley Gybletts (hence his cognomen of 'Gybletts' Chicken'). His opponent, Jem Brennan, a shoemaker also appearing for the first time in the prize-ring, had a good local reputation as a result of successes in private mills for love and glory.

The nomination of the place of combat had been left to *Bell's Life in London* which, besides being the most respected journal of the time for boxing affairs, also played an active role in facilitating the smooth running of various administrative matters. Since the newspaper was of the opinion that the majority of the spectators would be 'toddlers', it thought it would be "but charitable to shorten the trot of the poor soles as much as possible". Consequently, a convenient piece of ground was chosen close to the Swan with Two Necks but hidden from public view. There the supporters of both men crowded around the 24-foot arena while a score or so villagers risked life and limb in the stormy conditions by climbing nearby trees.

The contest commenced at one o'clock and first blood was drawn by the favourite Brennan, who at 34 was giving away 15 years to his taller opponent. However, by the end of the opening round, lasting nearly a quarter of an hour, Fitzmaurice had gained an advantage which he maintained throughout the 51-minute encounter. In the 23rd round, having severely punished the veteran about the head, he ended the bout with a cross-buttock throw which rendered Brennan totally senseless. The result caused acute embarrassment to the friends of the loser, who were so confident of his victory that printed accounts of his anticipated triumph were circulated before the true picture became apparent.

Successful Launch of the 'East End Sailor Boy'

Tom Smith, who by virtue of victories over Jack Adams and Barney Aaron could claim to be the best 10-stone fighter of the early 1830s, made his official début on 12 January 1829 against fellow novice Peter Smith. The venue for the bout, arranged for £5 a side, was at Whetstone in a field in front of the Swan with Two Necks. The encounter proved to be a determinedly contended one with the pugilists equally matched and showing admirable proficiency for such inexperienced men. Both were adept at stopping blows to the head so, although they favoured directing their attacks to that area, comparatively little facial damage was suffered.

Press coverage of the mill was very poor. *Bell's Life in London* merely reported the result and it was left to the *Weekly Dispatch* to print a few meagre details of the proceedings. However, this newspaper did not describe the way in which the battle was won, only that it had ended in favour of the "East End Chicken" (as it termed Tom Smith) after "a decent affair" lasting nearly an hour. *Bell's Life* was more specific in recording the length of the contest as 45 minutes and referred to the winner as the "East End Sailor Boy", the appellation by which Tom Smith became known throughout his subsequent career.

A second match, for £2 a side, followed between Tom Hurley, a protégé of Reuben Marten, and John Barber. Although the combatants were no more than minor bruisers, they participated in "a good stand up fight and science above mediocrity was displayed on both sides". Hurley showed himself to be the better man but, just when it appeared that his opponent would be forced to admit defeat, he was unlucky enough to fall awkwardly and sustain a badly strained ankle. This unfortunate injury compelled him to concede a victory which otherwise would undoubtedly have been his. The finale to the day's activities was a poor set-to between Bill M'Carthy and Jem Brasman, the latter being successful in winning the small purse of 12 shillings.

Ex-partner Bows to 'Sprig of Myrtle'

Ned Brown, inactive since his defeat by Solomon Reubens at Whetstone the previous year, returned to the village on 17 March 1829 to settle a dispute with his erstwhile partner in trade, Joe Bevan. The men had known each other since childhood, but whilst the 'Sprig' had mixed with some of the best lightweights of the time, Bevan had merely participated in a few bye-battles in his local neighbourhood. Consequently, despite giving away a considerable amount of weight to his former associate, Brown was installed as betting favourite.

The ragged horde, many shoeless, which made its way on that cold Tuesday morning up the (Great) North Road to the fight venue was buoyant and in good humour. Not surprisingly, it contained many London-based Irishmen, for what better way to celebrate St Patrick's Day than to attend a grudge mill. The Green Man at Whetstone was selected as Brown's headquarters whilst the 'Cock of Walham Green', as Bevan was known, chose the more modest setting of the Bull and Butcher. At these two hostelries the pugilists and their supporters remained until the time of the contest; since there was the inevitable demand for refreshments, both landlords had reason to be grateful for the disturbance about to take place in their midst.

At length, in a meadow at Bedstile (or Betstile), approximately half a mile to the east of Whetstone, a ring was formed and the participants set to. The encounter began in a cautious vein, which the *Weekly Dispatch* attributed to Brown being sensibly mindful of his opponent's physical advantages. *Bell's Life in London* took the opposite view and blamed Bevan who, it said, had won the toss for the choice of position, selected the high ground and was loath to come down. Brown eventually ended the first round impressively, delivering a heavy right hand on Bevan's left eye before moving in and forcing his man down. Dick Curtis, again in the 'Sprig's' corner, showed his delight and informed his charge that he was as good as ever. Ned soon began to take the lead, using his greater experience to negate the underdog's superior strength. By the 30th round Bevan had become so damaged about the face that, when he was knocked out of the ring, his backers ended his torment and Brown was proclaimed a worthy winner. The *Weekly Dispatch* summed up the event by commenting that "it is pleasing in these degenerative days of boxing to enlarge upon a fair and honest trial of skill and courage".

Following the match the loser, in a pitiful condition, was taken back to the Bull and Butcher. There, despite the large sums spent by his supporters earlier in the day, he was now refused entry. The excuse for this callous decision was that the hostess did not wish her abode to be turned into a hospital, and no amount of pleading by Bevan's worried friends could persuade her otherwise. They were therefore forced to transport the suffering fighter to Barnet where accommodation was finally found.

It is interesting to note that this occasion provided an early example of the amazing milling abilities of the legendary lightweight champion Owen Swift. The 'Little Wonder' was one of the most complete pugilists to appear in the prize-ring. Quick and accurate, he was equally adept at hitting or grappling and always exhibited excellent temperament, tactical awareness and 'bottom'. Just 15 years old at the time of the Brown–Bevan encounter, Swift and a friend were trudging along the road on their way to the fight when they were passed by a hackney-coach. Seeing a way to reach their destination more easily, the boys jumped on the back but were soon discovered. When they refused to get down, Tom Reidie stepped out of the coach to teach the pair a lesson. He was not, however, in peak form due to a surfeit of night life and soon gave up when he realized that, against the elusive young Swift, he had not a ghost of a chance. Those who witnessed the performance of the lithe teenager in the brief impromptu affair would not have been surprised at the heights he soon attained. Whetstone provided a happy hunting ground for Swift's precocious talents and, as will be seen, he scored several more successes in the area during the course of his dazzling career.

Fatal Milling

East Barnet was the site for the continuation of a contest on 18 March 1829 between Whitechapel's Arthur M'Ginnis, known by the honorary title of 'King of the Tinkers', and fellow Irishman Jack M'Daniels. The match, for £8 a side, had commenced in Wood Green near Green Lanes. However, following 32 uneventful rounds, intervention by "a Minister of Peace, in the form of a Constable" forced a hasty decampment. Hostilities were renewed in a muddy field at East Barnet where, after a further 62 rounds lasting one and a half hours, M'Ginnis gained the victory. This tedious encounter did little for the reputation of either man with M'Daniels succumbing more from exhaustion than from any punishment he had received. The winner finished the bout in such good shape that, after dressing, he returned to watch the second fight between his brother Jack and Hugh Doyle, a meeting which had fatal consequences for the former.

This second Irish battle, for £4 a side, was, according to the *Weekly Dispatch*, "contested with a vigour and manhood that would not have disgraced a contest for the championship". Doyle, a St Giles tinker, used an effective left hand with increasing regularity as the bout wore on and his opponent was forced to absorb sustained punishment to the head. M'Ginnis displayed considerable fortitude but after 28 rounds was rendered completely unconscious. He was taken back to Whitechapel where he expired at two o'clock the next morning, thus, as *Bell's Life in London* irreverently commented, "establishing his game by the sacrifice of his life".

A couple of days after the mill, a rumour circulated that an attempt had been made to snatch the body of the deceased which, because of his profession, could have been of interest to science. If this had been the case, the parties implicated in the tragedy would have benefited as no inquiry into the death could have taken place. However, the story proved to be false and an inquest was subsequently held on 21 March at the White Swan public house in Thrawl Street, Whitechapel. A coroner's jury brought in a verdict of manslaughter against Doyle, together with all four seconds involved, and warrants were then issued for their arrest.

'Sailor Boy' Drops Anchor at 'Little Tim's'

After seconding Charley Jones at Whetstone in May 1828, Harry Jones the 'Sailor Boy' suffered a distressing mishap whilst carrying his victorious cousin out of the ring. The *Weekly Dispatch* of 25 May reported that "poor Harry injured himself in a most severe and delicate manner. He is now under the hands of a surgeon and it is not likely that he will recover for a considerable time". However, Jones made a remarkable come-back in September and the following March was again to be found in the Barnet area. The occasion was the night before his contest

12. Harry Jones, the popular and enthusiastic 'Sailor Boy'

against Frank Redmond when the Bristolian reposed at 'Little Tim's' prior to securing a 10-round win at No Mans Land.

A few weeks later, when matched with George Watson at Harpenden Common, the 'Sailor Boy' returned to 'Little Tim's', this time using the inn for training purposes as well as a convenient pre-fight stopping place. There he was frequently visited by former champion Tom Spring and looked after by Tom 'Paddington' Jones, a widely respected veteran who 30 years previously had provided the opposition for Jem Belcher's first London appearance. Harry's adversary was himself a nephew of the illustrious Belchers. Watson's training at the Bell in Hendon was supervised by his uncle, Tom, who made the journey daily in a gig from his cottage on Finchley Common. On 19 May 1829, as a result of the diligent attention paid to the boxers, both entered the ring in peak condition with Jones proving the better man in a contest of 39 minutes' duration.

Harry Jones once more chose 'Little Tim's' as his training headquarters, again supervised by 'Paddington' Jones and Tom

Spring, in preparation for his 69-round victory over Dick Hill at Bagthorpe Common in June 1831. Sadly, at this point, his prolific career was nearly over and he died just four years later at the early age of 28. His claim to fistic celebrity, according to *Pugilistica*, came more from "the eminence of some of the men he contended with and did not beat, rather than the number of second-raters whose pretensions he disposed of". Miles, however, thereafter contradicted himself, and there can be no doubt that Jones, as he matured, recorded some excellent results. These included a victory over Jack Perkins, the only conqueror of Dick Curtis, revenge for three earlier losses to Ned Stockman and a 15-minute defeat of Barney Aaron. He was certainly good enough to earn the admiration of John Clare, the unfortunate peasant poet of the time, who later, during his long confinement in a lunatic asylum, occasionally believed that he was himself the 'Sailor Boy'.

A Fair Fight?

Ned Murphy, previously mentioned as James Burke's début opponent and known for his spirited sparring displays, met novice Tom Richardson for £10 a side on 23 June 1829. The contest, in a field about a mile from Whetstone, failed to attract many regular ring-goers although it was well attended by followers from the Marylebone and Paddington areas. These supporters, decidedly disreputable in appearance, converged on the village at an early hour and availed themselves copiously of the hospitality on tap at the Swan with Two Necks. The fighters themselves were also conveyed to this public house where, in separate rooms, they awaited the call to action.

Conceding all the physical advantages to the younger Murphy, Richardson put up a determined effort during the 42 minutes that the bout lasted. However, his first experience in the prize-ring proved a painful one as Murphy's accurate blows repeatedly found their intended target. Unable to inflict any damage on his more scientific adversary by legitimate means, the newcomer resorted to the use of head butts on several occasions. Unfortunately for him, he was no more adept at this tactic than he had been with his earlier offensive actions, whilst Murphy, when retaliating in kind, was far more effective. By the time his seconds gave in for him after 47 rounds, Richardson was severely bruised about the head and was taken from the scene in a distressed condition.

The *Weekly Dispatch* declared that "this was, beyond all doubt, a fair fight". Such a comment may appear surprising today but it must be remembered that the contest took place under the rudimentary and outmoded Broughton's Rules. Actions like butting, kicking, gouging and biting, although deemed morally wrong, were not specifically decreed fouls until the implementation of the 'New Rules' in 1838.

The 'Deaf'un' Disappoints

James Burke suffered his first defeat on 25 August 1829 when, on an extremely hot day at Whetstone, he yielded to the Chichester pugilist, Bill Cousens. This was perhaps the worst showing of Burke's eventful career and one in which his known eccentricity was much to the fore. In fact the *Weekly Dispatch* was at a total loss to explain his uncommitted performance, although its reporter was certain that the honesty of the 'Deaf'un' was never in doubt. Apart from insisting that no 'cross' had taken place, the paper was severely disparaging in its comments, whilst *Bell's Life in London* offered up the mistaken opinion that "neither of these men will ever cut a figure in the prize ring".

The much-criticized bout was fought in a meadow half a mile from the village (probably Bedstile) in front of a substantial crowd of some 10,000 people drawn to the occasion because of the recent dearth of milling activity. The protagonists appeared on the scene just before one o'clock and went to work shortly afterwards. For the most part the contest was of a scrambling nature and little punishment was meted out. Although Cousens sustained the most damage, Burke's lack of interest in the job at hand was periodically obvious. Eventually, after 2 hours 3 minutes of undistinguished action, the battle terminated in favour of the Chichester boxer.

It seems that there may have been some extenuating circumstances surrounding Burke's loss, for Henning tells us that he was foolhardy enough to walk the entire way from London to Whetstone. Such an act was scarcely the ideal preparation for an impending bout, especially in view of the oppressive weather. Furthermore the fighter was additionally handicapped by the effects of a rupture, which certainly could not have helped his cause against a naturally bigger opponent. The result proved only a temporary setback, however, for by the end of the year the 'Deaf'un' was back to winning ways.

13. The Chichester pugilist Bill Cousens, best known for his defeat of 'Deaf' Burke at Whetstone.

Cousens, meanwhile, trained at Kitts End the following month for his second successful match against Teddy Sweeney on 6 October. He prepared under the supervision of Robert Barclay-Allardice, better known as Captain Barclay, an innovative trainer whose major achievement in his long association with the prize-ring had been his conditioning of Tom Cribb for the champion's second victory over Tom Molineaux. Lineally descended from Robert II, the first Stewart (Stuart) King of Scotland, the captain was also a celebrated pedestrian, an eminent agriculturist, an officer in the Marquis of Huntly's Regiment of Gordon Highlanders and a noted whip.

Magistrates Hoodwinked

Solomon Reubens and Tom Smith were scheduled to appear at Whetstone, both for a second time, on 10 November 1829 in a match arranged for £10 a side. However, progress to the venue was interrupted when it was reported that the village was hosting a tithe dinner which was to be attended by certain magistrates known to be opposed to the fistic art. A meeting was therefore convened at the Green Man on Finchley Common, since it was felt that if the crowd continued their journey past the 'beaks' their worships would undoubtedly be alerted to the day's sport. The decision was taken to follow the proposals of the informant who had sounded the warning; he guided the cavalcade in a circular route by way of Colney Hatch Road (Lane), thus successfully skirting the hazardous locality.

About twelve o'clock a ring was formed on the ground originally intended, in Hungerford Lane (now Oakleigh Park North), within half a mile of Whetstone. The spectators numbered upwards of 2000 and included a large contingent of the Jewish supporters of Reubens who, over-confident of victory, were looking to bet heavily on their favourite. Soon afterwards the pugilists entered the arena, Reubens displaying a blood-red 'fogle' and the 'East End Sailor Boy' appropriately sporting one of navy blue. Neither had a significant weight advantage but Smith did have youth on his side.

From the 22nd round onwards it was obvious that the younger man had the upper hand, and by the 30th Reubens was labouring under the additional drawback of having lost the vision in his left eye. He nevertheless struggled on for five more rounds, at which point his seconds took the decision to retire him. It was, all agreed, a manly battle fought in a fair manner, with Smith demonstrating astonishing ring craft for a boxer who *Bell's Life in London* wrote, albeit mistakenly, was making his début.

Reubens had been the pre-fight favourite and his loss could certainly be attributed in part to the fact that he enjoyed a hedonistic lifestyle, preferring wine and women to the discipline of training. This propensity for the good life was to be responsible for his descent into crime and his resulting transportation on a charge of highway robbery. Indeed, when the *Glasgow Herald* later delighted in listing the considerable number of pugilists who had fallen foul of the law, it stated that Reubens was "long a celebrated thief and leader of thieves at the east end of the town [London]". Australia, however, must have had a favourable effect on him since in his obituary, in *Bell's Life in Sydney* (25 August 1849), Reubens was described as "a thoroughly honest and kindly disposed man".

No Go for Gow

On Monday 21 December 1829, at a gathering at Tom Cannon's public house in Jermyn Street, London, Whetstone was chosen as the venue where the promising young tyro Jack Gow would oppose Ned Savage the following day. However, Cannon was warned of possible magisterial interference and, on reaching the planned spot, a consultation was therefore held on whether to shift the scene of action beyond the jurisdiction of the Middlesex 'beaks'. Gow, so the *Weekly Dispatch* asserted, was eager to do battle at Whetstone since there were no signs of any apparent interruption, but the stakeholder insisted on moving on. The bout finally came off at No Mans Land with the novice winning easily in 23 rounds. Afterwards he alleged that his opponent had offered to throw the contest, not an unlikely scenario since, despite Savage's gameness, he was not averse to the odd nefarious dealing if it enhanced his financial position. (In fact, six months earlier he had feigned an injury and refused to enter the ring against John Davis, the 'Manchester Black', in an inexcusable attempt to rob his backer.)

The next year Gow fared no better in a further attempt to appear in the area. On this occasion the outcome proved far from favourable for him. He was matched on 23 February 1830 with a protégé of Jem Burn named Smith, but a posse of constables, backed up by mounted patrols, was determined that the fight should not go ahead. The would-be spectators were totally unaware of the situation. Hence, as *Bell's Life in London* (28 February) described the scene, "soon after daylight the road to Finchley was covered with travellers, the variety and miscellaneous characters of whose appearance was scarcely less singular than the 'turn-out' in Hogarth's celebrated March of the same direction".

Having reached Whetstone, the rabble halted at the Swan with Two Necks where one of the villagers delivered a warning that two horse patrols were primed to prevent the impending encounter. It was thus decided to move the bout further afield. Eventually Tom Oliver, the commissary of the prize-ring in charge of the ropes and stakes, located and took possession of a suitable site. At this juncture the cavalry, which rather surprisingly had followed unnoticed, suddenly appeared and bore down on the unsuspecting throng. The unfortunate Jack Gow and a friend of his by the name of Cummings were both taken prisoner and conveyed to Bow Street, where they were bound over to keep the peace in their own personal recognizances of £20.

Burke Storms to Victory

The Fancy never allowed personal discomfort to interfere with their viewing of a well-planned day's sport, and often endured considerable hardship in order to attend any match-up promising to result in a sanguinary conflict. Hence, despite ferocious storms on 16 November 1830, *Bell's Life in London* expressed no surprise that "the road towards Barnet presented a lively sprinkle of connoisseurs". The occasion was yet another fight in the early career of James Burke, the destination being Whetstone where a meeting between the 'Deaf'un' and Tim Crawley had been arranged. The 13-stone Crawley, a 23-year-old coal-whipper, had earned a minor reputation in several private confrontations. Having been unimpressed with Burke's performance against Bob Hampson three weeks earlier, he had persuaded his friends to back him in this trial.

By noon a ring had been erected on rising ground in a field close to the village. Here, *Bell's Life* recounted, "the whistling wind had ample opportunity to play its vagaries in carrying off umbrellas, untiling the nobs of the fresh coves, and occasionally unseating those high minded folks, who had got perched on top of a 'jarvey' or the seat of a taxed cart". As the combatants came up to scratch, the knowing members of the large crowd could not fail to notice the awkward bearing of the long-limbed muscular novice; there was a distinctly unprofessional look about him whilst the compact frame of the 'Deaf'un' denoted superior strength.

The first round clearly demonstrated the degree to which Crawley had overestimated his chances of victory. His initial charge was met with two hard blows to the head and Burke continued to hammer away spiritedly before throwing his man heavily. Fortunately for the coal-whipper, the soft earth reduced the amount of concussion he suffered but the effects of his opponent's sharp hitting could plainly be seen on his face. He continued to take a tremendous amount of punishment during the next four rounds, although his bold rushes did produce the occasional success. In the fifth he even managed to draw blood from Burke's nose but thereafter the battle was all one way. Despite Crawley's extra weight and excellent endurance, he had little idea how to utilize these physical attributes or cope with the effective style of the masterful 'Deaf'un'. In the 34th round, nearly blind in both eyes and with his countenance fearfully swollen, Crawley was carried, strongly protesting, out of the ring.

At the conclusion of the 30-minute main contest both the participants and their seconds were thoroughly soaked and covered in mud whilst the ring itself had been transformed into a complete quagmire. This did not prevent preparations from immediately taking place for the second bout on the agenda, a lightweight encounter featuring two men known to the Fancy for the ability they had exhibited at Jem Burn's sparring school. The adverse conditions notwithstanding, Sam Gilpin and Fred Painter treated those present to an accomplished display of rapid hitting, stopping and countering which led the *Bell's Life* reporter to eulogize that he had witnessed "thirty as pretty rounds as ever graced the Annals of the Ring". At the start Gilpin scored with a dreadful strike on his adversary's cheekbone, which caused it to swell alarmingly, and for the remainder of the mill he continued to impress with the quality of his punches. Painter's returns were no less damaging and Gilpin also did not escape injury. Ultimately, though, the latter's better stamina and superior tactical brain enabled him to register a polished début victory.

The day concluded with a strange incident involving the deputy commissary, Jack Fogo, a former tailor known as 'Frosty Faced' Fogo because of his pockmarked features. Considered the poet laureate of the prize-ring, his poems could often be found in contemporary newspapers and he was a great attraction in London's numerous low-life drinking dens where he would frequently recite his works. Fogo, it seemed, had quarrelled with trainer Tommy Roundhead about either the origins of a Greek verb or the literary capabilities of the renowned ex-bruiser and toper Jack Scroggins, and wished to settle this grave dispute in fistic fashion. His official duties completed, Fogo called for Roundhead to join him in the ring and soon afterwards the trainer appeared stripped to the waist and ready for action. The deputy commissary himself then began to peel off his clothes. Much to the disappointment of the majority of the spectators, however, he was interrupted by the sport's aristocracy who had decided that it was unbecoming for "so distinguished a character to descend from Parnassus upon so unworthy an occasion". Fogo was therefore forced to decline the contest and the drenched and bedraggled mob, deprived of an amusing finale to the proceedings, began to wend their way back through the mud towards the metropolis.

'East End Sailor Boy' Sinks M'Carthy

The 'East End Sailor Boy' Tom Smith, still unbeaten and having registered a win over 16-year-old Owen Swift since his last Whetstone appearance, again displayed his talents in the area on Tuesday 22 March 1831. Termed a "rising star" by the press of the time, Smith was matched for £25 a side against the competent Jem M'Carthy, a neat scientific boxer who was taller and a few pounds heavier than the favourite. Both men trained in the vicinity of Barnet and, on the morning of the contest, a field to the east of Whetstone was selected as the site for the confrontation. *Bell's Life in London* described how this "was soon thronged by anxious spectators whose impatience was in some measure subdued by occasional 'drops of brandy' as well as 'drops of gin' which, spite the terrors of the Excise, were sold without licence in no mean quantities".

Once the area around the ring had been cleared, the fighters made their entrance. It was immediately apparent that the pair were in superb physical shape. The bout, however, proved to be a major disappointment to those who had been eagerly anticipating a competitive spectacle. It was soon obvious that M'Carthy was unable to cope with his opponent's powerful onslaughts and by round ten 'Young Dutch Sam', who had initially backed the underdog, could be observed frantically trying to lay off his bet in a futile attempt to cut his losses. Smith's strength grew as the battle progressed whilst M'Carthy's confidence quickly ebbed away and it could hardly have helped the latter's morale when, at the end of the 16th round, he saw the 'Sailor Boy' disdaining the opportunity to rest on his second's knee. A round later Peter Crawley, in M'Carthy's corner, took the decision to put an end to the increasingly one-sided action after his battered charge had complained of internal injuries. When he was removed from the ring, it was found that the loser had sustained three broken ribs, which totally vindicated the humane judgment of the former champion. Smith, meanwhile, accepted the congratulations for a job well done and the unusually disciplined rabble prepared themselves for a purse fight between two 'outsiders' named Nowlan and Coakley.

Paddy Nowlan was the cause of much merriment since his extremely bony frame gave him the appearance of a living skeleton. Banter about his extraordinary physique was rife and it was generally agreed that he must have been "prigged from a bone yard". However, once the mill began Nowlan's gameness and boxing ability soon earned him the respect of the previously derisive spectators. His adversary, Mike Coakley, was a busy well-schooled fighter and the two were involved in a spirited, albeit brief, affair which afforded considerable entertainment. It culminated in a ninth-round victory for the stronger man after Nowlan had been the recipient of severe punishment.

Not Gilpin's Afternoon

In front of a select gathering of the Fancy the 'Pocket Hercules', Anthony Noon, had his second ring engagement when he exhibited at Whetstone on 26 April 1831. The scene of the action had not been divulged until the previous day in the hope that many of the lower order would be prevented from attending. Even at this early stage of his career Noon was attracting considerable attention and the *Weekly Dispatch* deemed the defensive abilities he demonstrated to be reminiscent of the science displayed by Tom Spring during his heyday a few years earlier.

The 'Pocket Hercules' was brought forward under the auspices of Tom Gaynor, himself no mean performer of the noble art and the conqueror of men of the confirmed calibre of Ned Neale and Alec Reid. Gaynor, assisted by 'Young Dutch Sam', seconded his protégé against the challenge of the skilful Sam Gilpin. The latter, who had made a sparkling début at Whetstone some six months previously, had trained for this bout at an inn on the Barnet road. He had Jem Burn as his patron and was looked after by the 'Sailor Boy', Harry Jones. The fighters, in excellent fettle, weighed about 8 stone 4 pounds for the contest; Gilpin had the slight edge in height whilst Noon was physically the stronger.

Both boxers were extremely cautious at the start but, at length, Noon got the better of a sharp exchange of punches and followed this by throwing his man. The next three rounds were critical for, during this period, Gilpin received several hard right-hand blows which had the effect of completely closing his left eye. In the fifth round Noon again found the target with a severe strike "which nearly cut the flesh from the lower covering of the glistener and excited great alarm for the sight of the eye itself". However, he was unable to inflict much further damage since he sustained an injury to the knuckles of his right hand and his work with the left proved to be mostly ineffectual. Gilpin, for his part, could not take advantage of his adversary's restricted options since Noon's skill at blocking or moving away from attacks remained unimpaired. In addition the 'Pocket Hercules' dominated in close, where he repeatedly succeeded in throwing Gilpin heavily before falling with his full weight upon him.

Eventually it became obvious to Burn that his fighter, although still relatively fresh, had no chance of combating Noon's supremacy, especially whilst sporting such a horrendous eye injury. He therefore interposed after 2 hours 13 minutes of extended hostilities during which 54 rounds had been completed.

Ex-convict Makes Good

Jack Adams, who during his meritorious career mixed with some of the best lighter men of the period, encountered one Jerry Donovan at Cockfosters, a short distance from Barnet, on 9 August 1831. According to the *Licensed Victuallers' Gazette*, Adams had been sentenced as a youth to seven years on board the Chatham hulks, but earned a free pardon by single-handedly plugging a leak which was causing his floating prison to sink. At the time of the Donovan fight he was 26 years old. He had recently defeated Young Richmond whose father, the renowned Bill Richmond, was the first American to achieve fame in the bareknuckle arena.

Donovan won the toss to choose the right of venue and originally opted for Colney Heath. However, on the day of the bout, the location was changed to Cockfosters since this was nearer the Green Man in Whetstone where he had stopped for the night. Adams, who had been staying at the Green Man on Finchley Common, also made his way to the new site. There a ring had been formed on a "beautiful piece of common" at the extremity of the village. Although the 'toddlers', commanded by the indefatigable Jack Scroggins, were not as numerous as had been expected, there were nevertheless "two thousand anxious mugs" on the scene by the time the pugilists entered the field of combat. Donovan's seconds were Dick Curtis and Harry Jones whilst Adams was attended by Ben Burn, the uncle of his mentor, Jem Burn, and 'Young Dutch Sam'.

Having cordially shaken hands, the participants were soon ready for action and, at eleven minutes to one, were led to the scratch. Both protagonists were around the 10-stone mark with Donovan being slightly the bigger of the two. Adams, though, was by far the better boxer and his tactical ability, allied to the speed and precision of his blows, gave him a decided edge. He gained both first knock-down and first blood in the second round and, despite severely cutting his finger on Donovan's teeth in the tenth, continued to punish his man heavily. The contest lasted for 36 minutes; when Adams stepped up his attack in the 17th round his opponent's friends, realizing the futility of prolonging Donovan's suffering, conceded the fight.

The match which followed saw Sam Gilpin give away height and weight to the stronger Bill Isaacs in a mill arranged for £5 a side. Isaacs made maximum use of his superior advantages and, in the course of the 14-round battle, knocked out three of his adversary's teeth as well as fracturing his jaw in two places. The entertainment having passed off satisfactorily, the road home was a scene of "lively frolick [*sic*]" and included the several private roadside set-tos customary after such an occasion. The day had tragic consequences for Gilpin, however, who subsequently expired at Middlesex Hospital 15 days later. His death was attributed to a cold caught in the aftermath of the contest whilst in a state of perspiration.

'Westminster Pet' Retires Richmond's Boy

An interesting confrontation occurred at Whetstone on 4 October 1831 when the 'Westminster Pet', Byng Stocks, met Young Richmond for £5 a side. Stocks, a bricklayer making his first boxing appearance, was under the patronage of the well-known Charles Alstropp, a staunch supporter of the sport. His opponent, since his father's death, had obtained a livelihood by teaching sparring; he had fought just once before, this being the loss inflicted on him at Colney Heath by Jack Adams earlier that year. The men both weighed about 10 stone 8 pounds but, while Richmond was tall and lean, Stocks was much shorter and of muscular build.

On arriving at the village it was realized that no ropes and stakes were available. Tom Oliver had yet to return from Doncaster races and his assistant, Jack Fogo, was touring the northern counties. However, as the two parties were quite prepared to go ahead without the customary enclosure, this did not prove to be a major obstacle. In the appointed field a large ring was formed around which the surprisingly well-behaved spectators grouped themselves, and shortly before one o'clock the hostilities began. At the onset Richmond was able to utilize his superior reach and had the decided advantage with his long shots. Stocks, realizing that he had no hope of winning the contest at a distance, was forced to resort to aggressive charges, frequently forcing his man down and falling heavily upon him. This tactic proved so successful in weakening Richmond that, much to the delight of the Westminster Fancy, he was forced to admit defeat after 74 arduous rounds lasting 1 hour 18 minutes.

Whilst the winner used the victory as a springboard for a successful career, Richmond never entered the ring again. Sporting history records many instances of sons failing to emulate the achievements of their famous fathers, and Young Richmond was a noted early example of this trend.

Mob Forces the Issue

"As the battle is small in amount and the betting not extensive, we think there is a chance, for once in a way, of a fair fight – if the magistrates do not interfere". So commented the *Weekly Dispatch* (18 December 1831) on the subject of a forthcoming match-up between the two capable lightweights Bill Isaacs and Sam Hinton. Unfortunately, the paper was mistaken in its optimism, for the affair was marked by disgraceful conduct on the part of a mob adamant that Isaacs should not have the slightest opportunity of success.

The mill, for £10 a side, was arranged for Tuesday 20 December and the toss for choice of venue was won by Hinton who decided on the neighbourhood of Whetstone. On the arrival of commissary

Tom Oliver at the village with the ropes and stakes, a field close to the Swan with Two Necks was selected as the site of the contest. Before long, rumours began circulating that a warrant had been issued by a Middlesex and Hertfordshire magistrate directing officers to prevent a breach of the peace. This was believed by some sceptics to be unfounded, but to their dismay a constable shortly appeared with the offending document. Hinton and his friends, having learnt of the situation, deemed it sensible to continue on to Cockfosters. There they heard that Oliver and Isaacs had made their way, by a circuitous route, to a spot two miles further on. However, when they reached the said location no sign of a ring could be found and, to add to their frustration, it was realized that they had been followed by two tenacious 'traps'. A return towards London was therefore agreed upon, but at East Barnet a messenger sent by the commissary overtook them and announced that Isaacs was waiting in a meadow within half a mile of Whetstone.

Meanwhile the crowd that had already arrived organized an impromptu bout between Tom M'Keevor, later described by the *Licensed Victuallers' Gazette* as a "game and sturdy little Irishman", and a St Giles man, Tom Berry (Barry). A purse of 25 shillings was on offer to the winner, and was claimed by M'Keevor after a resolute and courageous effort by both bruisers.

By the time Hinton reached the ground Isaacs had been waiting for over two hours and, not surprisingly in view of the typical December weather, was shivering violently from head to foot. Even then there was a further obstacle to overcome before the action could finally get under way. One of the 'traps' forced his way to the ropes where, in routine fashion, he called on Oliver, in the King's name, to assist in preserving the peace. The commissary, aware that the King was in Brighton and would not be overly concerned with such matters, declined to answer the call. The constable was lifted off his feet and unceremoniously bundled out of the ring, at which point he prudently made the decision to retire from the scene.

With daylight fast disappearing the pugilists were at last brought to the scratch. Seconding Hinton were Jack Adams and the commissary himself. Supporting his opponent were the recently retired top-class lightweight Jack Tisdale and a butcher named Carter. Hinton, an elegant boxer, had the advantage in height and reach but the solid muscular Isaacs was clearly the heavier man.

For 24 rounds the encounter was fairly evenly contested; both exhibited excellent knowledge of the fistic science, with Hinton showing himself to be the more confident performer and Isaacs the stronger.

At this point an unruly mob, heavily prejudiced against Isaacs, began to make its ugly presence felt. *Bell's Life in London* was convinced that the campaign was waged because the crowd mistakenly believed Isaacs to be Jewish. However, it was more likely due to the greater sum of money that had been betted on Hinton. Whatever the reason, there can be little doubt that the underdog was forced to fight in circumstances hardly conducive to success. Violent threats were continually made in an effort to convince him to give in, and on one occasion he was even struck with a heavy whip across his naked torso. The *Weekly Dispatch* likened the situation to that which had occurred just three months earlier at the infamous second bout between Tom Brown and Phil Sampson. That shameful affair had terminated when Brown, his life in danger from supporters of his antagonist, was taken from the ring for his own safety.

Ignoring the crowd's growing anger at his refusal to concede the contest, Isaacs, his stamina waning but his resolve still strong, continued stubbornly to prolong the struggle. In the 40th round the *Bell's Life* reporter, increasingly unsettled by the intimidating atmosphere, elected to abandon his task and quietly take his leave. "The impatience of the throng being every moment more strongly manifested against Isaacs", a few rounds later Jack Tisdale made the decision to give in for his man and Hinton was carried out of the ring in triumph. The correct duration of the battle cannot be ascertained. *Bell's Life* (1 hour 35 minutes) and the *Weekly Dispatch* (2 hours 30 minutes) were at variance whilst other newspapers did not consider the bout significant enough for inclusion.

The retreat back to town was hampered by darkness, and some of the exuberant horde, while negotiating their way to the main road, found themselves immersed in ditches full of muddy water. The most notable casualty was a far from sober Jack Scroggins (he once estimated that he consumed 40 glasses of gin daily) who was discovered by a minister half submerged and sound asleep in a deep slough. The unfortunate Scroggins, his days as a pugilistic hero long gone, was at this stage of his life a pitiful character reliant on charity from the Fancy in order to survive. He was extricated with difficulty from what nearly proved a muddy grave and, after being fortified with yet more alcohol, was pointed in the direction of the metropolis which he reached safely early next morning.

Three days afterwards, at the Red Horse in Bond Street, the stake money was given up to Hinton. The action elicited a protest from an aggrieved Isaacs who believed that it was only Tisdale's fear of the angry mob which caused his second to resign the contest. Since the *Weekly Dispatch* reporter wrote that he heard Tisdale remark to his charge "it is of no use – they will not let you win", Isaacs obviously had strong grounds

14. Jack Scroggins, a doughty warrior and renowned toper

for complaint. Many people, in consequence of the foul play involved, declared their intention of not honouring their bets. The loser, for his part, challenged Hinton to another match, this time for £25 pounds a side. Although the latter agreed in principle to a fresh meeting, the return does not appear to have taken place.

A 'Snip' Cleans Up at the 'Dirt House'

A minor battle for £5 a side between two bruisers from the capital's 'back slums', Joe Woodhouse, a tailor, and Dan Mahoney, a cabman of Irish extraction, was decided on Monday 13 February 1832. A report in the following Sunday's edition of *Bell's Life in London* related that "Whetstone was at first intended as the scene of the action but the beaks were 'wide awake' in that quarter; the toddlers having had a hint pulled up at the 'Dirt-house' on the Finchley-road". This tavern was the Old White Lion, located on the site where the present building, bearing the same name, stands today, on the Great North Road near East Finchley station. It acquired the alternative appellation of the 'Dirt House' when it became a favourite stopping place of the carters who transported hay into the metropolis and manure and soot out again.

The 'Sailor Boy', Harry Jones, selected a field to the rear of the Old White Lion as a suitable spot for the mill and an open ring was quickly formed. Jones himself seconded the tailor, together with Jack Adams's former victim, Jerry Donovan, whilst two men named Shea and Battie performed the same task for Mahoney. Although neither fighter exhibited any great degree of skill they both demonstrated considerable courage, especially the cabman who was forced to absorb some dreadful blows to the body. The contest lasted for 1 hour 15 minutes during which, at one stage, the ring was broken into and chaos ensued. At the end of this time, with Mahoney having received a severe battering, Woodhouse was pronounced the winner. The defeated 'knight of the whip' was immediately put to bed, but swiftly recovered and was able to return to London the same night.

15. 'The Mail Coach Changing Horses' at the Old White Lion, Finchley.
Engraving (1825) after an original by James Pollard.
(Reproduced by kind permission of Barnet Local Studies and Archives.)

Dual Preparations at Finchley

In March 1832 the Green Man on Finchley Common was selected as the training headquarters for Anthony Noon and Jack Adams. The dual arrangement came about since both men had fights arranged within a week of one another and were from the same boxing stable, being Jem Burn's protégés. Noon, preparing for his meeting on 27 March with Owen Swift, and Adams, due to face Tom Smith on 3 April, were looked after by Tom Callas. This well-respected trainer made certain that his charges entered their contests in peak condition. Neither pugilist, however, proved successful. In two long-drawn-out bouts at Colney Heath, Noon was disqualified for an unintentional foul whilst Adams eventually succumbed to his unbeaten adversary after a most desperate conflict.

Two years later the pair attempted to avenge these losses with widely differing results. Noon, the 'Pocket Hercules', made a courageous effort to turn the tables on Swift at Andover on 24 June 1834. This had fatal repercussions, with the former tragically dying following a gruelling encounter lasting 2 hours 6 minutes. Adams fared significantly better and was responsible for the first-ever defeat inflicted upon the 'East End Sailor Boy' when they clashed again at Green Street Green in Kent on 21 October of the same year.

Swift too Speedy for Heavier Hobbs

Owen Swift's official Whetstone début was on 23 May 1832 against a butcher by the name of Hobbs. The 'Little Wonder', still only 18, was fresh from his first victory over the redoubtable Anthony Noon eight weeks earlier, and took the contest merely to keep in practice whilst awaiting further opportunities to move up the fistic ladder.

Hobbs was by far the bigger man but Swift succeeded in easily nullifying his two-stone weight disadvantage by virtue of superior speed and accurate hitting. In fact the teenage phenomenon proved so effective that the bout, whilst a spirited one, lasted a mere seven minutes during which five rounds were fought. This probably came as a great relief to Swift who, having taken a lengthy 2 hours 10 minutes to quell Noon's gallant challenge, would hardly have relished another arduous fight in such a short space of time.

Duo from St Giles

The previously referred to district of London called St Giles was one of the country's most infamous and squalid slums at a time when overcrowded lawless rookeries were rife in urban England. Notorious for its teeming and highly active criminal community, it lay between the churches of St Giles and St George, Bloomsbury, with a central core extending from St Giles High Street to Great Russell Street. (St George's church can be seen in the background of Hogarth's 'Gin Lane', which portrayed a disturbing picture of the area in the middle of the 18th century.) Not surprisingly, in view of the depravity and deprivation associated with this particular locality, St Giles produced more than its fair share of second-rate bruisers, in addition to several more renowned boxers such as Tom Smallwood, 'Deaf' Burke and the 'Nonpareil', Jack Randall. Amongst those in the first category were two brave but limited battlers called Bryan and Murray who were matched, for £5 a side, at Whetstone on Tuesday 13 November 1832.

Although the contest had little significance, both fighters were supported by well-known pugilists. Some six and a half months after their first epic confrontation, Owen Swift and Anthony Noon faced each other as opposing seconds. Swift was in the corner of the lighter man, Murray, who at a little over 10 stone was giving away 36 pounds to Noon's charge, Bryan. Despite the considerable weight disparity, Murray was able to prolong the ferocious conflict for 55 minutes by which time, totally spent, he was compelled to cry 'enough'.

A Full Day's Entertainment

Swift was back at Whetstone a week later when he drew a large crowd for his encounter, for £10 a side, with Jem Collins, a novice from South London. The majority of the spectators had deserted the 'back slums' of the metropolis to be present for the day, but Swift's rapidly increasing reputation also attracted a small gathering of Corinthians, together with ring celebrities such as Tom Spring, Tom Cannon and Dick Curtis.

Once the contest began the enormous gulf between the two men, in both class and experience, immediately became apparent. Collins, although the bigger man, was so completely outmatched that he was scarcely able to land a blow of any consequence throughout the 27 minutes that the fight lasted. Swift demonstrated his full range of talents as he totally dominated with a busy two-handed approach and scored repeatedly with precise punches. He was also increasingly effective with frequent heavy cross-buttock throws, and the one-sided bout should have been terminated long before the brave Collins was knocked senseless in the 21st round. Whilst his opponent was carried unconscious from the ring, the victor dressed quickly on the spot and settled down to view the continuing entertainment.

After 'Young Dutch Sam' had managed to raise £3 1s from the assembled company, two minor bruisers then entered the ring to compete for this purse. Tom Evans, the favourite, was a pump-borer from Lambeth, where he had a solid reputation amongst the local fistic community. He was opposed by Tom Berry, known in the Barnet area for the game effort he had put up against Tom M'Keevor 11 months previously. *Bell's Life in London* (25 November) waxed lyrical about this hastily arranged affair, even going so far as to state "a better purse fight we have scarce ever witnessed". Certainly there was enough punishment meted out on both sides to satisfy the most seasoned members of the Fancy, and a pleasing degree of science was also in evidence. Evans took the lead in the first few rounds but Berry bided his time and in the seventh succeeded in closing his adversary's left eye. Thereafter the contest was in the balance until, after 50 minutes, the Lambeth man became so exhausted that he was unable to continue. Much of the credit for Berry's unexpected victory was due to Anthony Noon, whose expert demonstration of the art of seconding was largely responsible for sustaining his tiring charge.

The day's official sport was then at a close but, to the delight of those watching, two itinerant gin-sellers proceeded to fight a pitched battle using the empty jars which had earlier contained their wares. Having vigorously tested the hardness of their crowns for several minutes, *Bell's Life* reported that they "concluded by crying most woefully over the fragments of their bottles and the bumps on their pericraniums". (Gin happened to be the favourite tipple of the Fancy, being known by various names of which 'daffy' was the most used. The drink even gave its name to the famous Daffy Club which met at Tom Belcher's Castle Tavern in Holborn; amongst the founder members and leading lights was Pierce Egan, who wrote its official song. One of the club's main purposes, apart from the consumption of excessive amounts of gin, was to "keep the 'GAME *alive*'".)

Thompson Tames 'Jaw Breaker'

The unfortunate Ned Thompson, shortly to suffer an untimely end at Whetstone, opposed one Joe Tibbett in a field near the village on Wednesday 2 January 1833. A baker nicknamed the 'Paddington Pet', Thompson was a brave and determined competitor; of Tibbett little is known except that some time previously he had acquired "the expressive and honourable cognomen of 'the Jaw Breaker'". Tibbett had the advantage of being attended by Harry Jones, whose considerable ring experience meant that he was much in demand in this capacity. Thompson, meanwhile, had to rely on the services of Ned Stockman's less regarded brother, Jem.

The battle, which was for £5 a side, comprised 18 hard-fought rounds lasting a total of 50 minutes. Tibbett's contribution was a valiant one but he sustained a severe beating before finally being knocked under. The loser left the ground in a badly bruised condition, in marked contrast to the fresh appearance of Thompson who exhibited few scars of battle.

Waterman Damps Down Pulser's Challenge

A dispute over a member of the fair sex led to a set-to at Whetstone on Tuesday 22 January 1833 between Bill Harris the Waterman and a novice by the name of Sam Pulser. Harris, who had participated in several ring battles had, *Bell's Life in London* related, "made too free with the inamorata of Pulser". This resulted in the latter unwisely demanding a contest for £10 a side and the favours of the lady in question. Although neither man had a major reputation, the affair obviously captured the imagination of the prize-fighting fraternity since they turned up in large numbers to see the quarrel settled. Harris had knowledgeable support in the form of the 'Sailor Boy', Harry Jones, and also Jerry Donovan who, despite being unsuccessful in his pugilistic career, did earn a measure of recognition as a second and trainer. Pulser was waited on by Jack Nicholls and Bob Coates, themselves fighting men, and the celebrated Dick Curtis took on the role of time-keeper.

Neither of the combatants had a weight advantage, both being about 9 stone 4 pounds, but not surprisingly Harris showed himself to be the superior from the opening exchanges. He concentrated on belabouring his opponent's head with a considerable amount of venom whilst Pulser attempted to work principally to the body and in close always fell undermost. The novice did rally after the 18th round, although to no avail since he was unable to make any of his blows tell effectively. He continued to be on the receiving end of a severe thrashing until the 35th round when weakness completely overcame him and he failed to make it up to the scratch.

Harris, scarcely marked and now as successful in war as in love, departed in high spirits while the loser, attempting to explain away his costly defeat, complained of being drugged. There can be no question that 'hocussing' did occasionally take place within the sport, especially when vast sums of money could be won or lost on the performance of a favoured bruiser. However, it is most unlikely in this case that Pulser's defeat could be attributed to anything other than his rival's greater ability.

Swift Again

Yet another appearance at Whetstone for Owen Swift saw him take on the heavier and better conditioned Jack Allen ("a 'rum un' from Saffron-hill"), on 5 February 1833, in front of 3000 fervent spectators. The 'Little Wonder' looked fatigued after the first 12 rounds of hits and counter-hits, but excellent work by his seconds, Dick Curtis and 'Gipsy' Cooper, always enabled him to come to the scratch ready to fight anew. Experience accrued beyond his tender years also allowed the lighter Swift to husband his strength carefully whilst still managing "to administer lots of pepper". Meanwhile Allen resolutely persevered in the hope that the favourite would irrevocably weaken. However, it was not to be and by the 41st round his supporters, seeing no chance of ultimate glory, were of the opinion that the contest should be ended. Harry Jones carried out their wishes and gave in for his man, but the fighter would not accept defeat and completed a further three rounds before his followers broke into the ring. At that point referee Peter Crawley and the umpires agreed to terminate the bout despite a claim from Allen's father that his son was capable of continuing. The loser's bravery so impressed the large gathering that the 'Streatham Youth', Ned Neale, was able to collect the sum of nearly £5 to assuage the disappointed Allen's suffering. The battle lasted 1 hour 40 minutes and *Bell's Life in London* aptly summed it up with the words "superior science was here opposed with its usual success to game and superior strength".

Following that entertainment came a mill between two men who had both previously contended at Whetstone, Westminster's Byng Stocks and St Giles bruiser Tom Berry. The latter had prepared at 'Little Tim's' in Kitts End for the engagement. Nevertheless, no amount of conditioning could compensate for his bigger opponent's greater fighting abilities and the brave underdog was comprehensively outclassed. Despite the careful attentions of his second, Dick Curtis, Berry could do little other than absorb punishment. After being knocked down for the 20th time, he sensibly decided that discretion was the better part of valour and withdrew from the contest.

Both victor and vanquished continued to have links with the Barnet area during their subsequent careers. At the beginning of 1835 Stocks trained under Jack Clarke at the Five Bells, Finchley, prior to a bout with Liverpool's Harry Woods ('Young Spring'). Woods was an excellent conjuror and ventriloquist but his talents failed to stretch to the fistic art (the *Licensed Victuallers' Gazette* described him as a "wretched boxer") and when the two met Stocks emerged a predictably easy winner. Three years later, again looked after by Jack Clarke, the 'Westminster Pet' repaired to a "quaint little inn on the Barnet Road" in readiness for his unsuccessful challenge against the formidable John 'Hammer' Lane, one of only two pugilists to have defeated Owen Swift. The experienced Clarke was also responsible for overseeing Berry's conditioning regime at a training house "just outside Barnet" before the St Giles man defeated Patsy M'Nolty on 30 May 1837 at Colney Heath.

Returning to Swift, the Allen encounter proved to be the last occasion that he exhibited his extraordinary talent in the area. However, in February 1834, as recognized champion of the lightweights, he did stay at the Green Man, Finchley, whilst preparing for his meeting with Bill Atkinson. The match resulted in another victory for the 'Little Wonder' but from then on his milling career was to be shrouded in tragedy. Besides the death of Anthony Noon after their second contest, for which he was sentenced to six months' incarceration in Winchester Castle, Swift

16. The legendary lightweight Owen Swift, whose illustrious career was shrouded in tragedy.

was also responsible for the demise of William Phelps in March 1838. This unfortunate occurrence left him in the unenviable position of being the only prize-ring champion to have killed two of his opponents, and led to the introduction of the 'New Rules' designed to bring greater safety and order to the sport. Swift sought refuge in France but was sentenced to 13 months' imprisonment by the Paris Tribunal of Correction for having participated in a fight there with Jack Adams. By that time he had fled back to

England and at his subsequent trial at the Hertford Assizes was acquitted of Phelps's manslaughter. He became landlord of the Horseshoe in the Haymarket which he turned into one of London's most popular sporting houses, but towards the end of his life adversity again overtook him. Destitute and in ill-health, Swift ended his days at the Licensed Victuallers' Asylum in the Old Kent Road where he died, aged 65, on 9 June 1879.

The Lesser-known Molineaux

The name Molineaux has an honoured place in the annals of boxing due to the exploits of the former American slave who twice grappled with Tom Cribb for the championship of England. However, 'Young Molineaux', whose star in the fistic firmament shone as brightly as the earlier celebrated Tom Molineaux, is today practically unknown except by those especially conversant with the bareknuckle era. This is despite the fact that he remained unbeaten in contests with some of the best 11-stone men of his day. Indeed Harry Cleveland, a respected journalist and author, even went as far as to write in his 1924 publication, *Fisticuffs and Personalities of the Prize Ring*, that he was "perhaps the best coloured pugilist of any time".

Born James Wharton, 'Young Molineaux' was also dubbed 'Jemmy the Black' and the 'Moroccan Prince', the last nickname arising since he originally hailed from Tangier. At a young age he became a cabin boy on a ship sailing to and from the East Indies and, on the long voyages, impressed both passengers and officers alike with his milling abilities. Advised to seek his fortune in the ring, he went to London where his début match was arranged by 'Pea Green' Hayne, a well-known sporting gentleman, against whom the actress Maria Foote had once recovered substantial damages in a breach-of-promise action. Hayne, the former backer of Tom Cannon and Ned Baldwin, lined up Tom M'Keevor as the novice's first antagonist and the bout came off in a field near Whetstone on 16 April 1833.

M'Keevor, seconded by Cannon and Anthony Noon, enjoyed an advantage in experience and also condition for, unlike 'Young Molineaux', he had been properly trained for the occasion. The latter's lack of fitness showed several times during the 38-round battle but, skilfully attended by Dick Curtis and Jack Adams, he was still able to produce a lively performance that highlighted his obvious potential. Round one ended with him throwing his man heavily, and he afterwards succeeded in drawing first blood and obtaining the first knock-down. An incensed M'Keevor attempted to exact retribution by introducing head butts into his strategy, which encouraged Wharton to adopt similar tactics. This resulted, to the great amusement of the spectators, in one particular incident when "they both rammed at the same time, and rebounded from each other with the noise of a couple of detonators bursting". Although 'Young Molineaux' often reduced the effect of his punches by striking with his hands open, he still connected with enough damaging blows to secure his maiden victory after 54 minutes of clever fighting.

Following wins over Evans, the 'Herefordshire Pippin', and Wil(l)sden, the 'Hammersmith Cowboy', a match was made with future champion Nick Ward (whose own connections with the Barnet area will be chronicled shortly). The contest was scheduled for Moulsey Hurst on 12 May 1835, and Wharton went into training at Finchley under the direction of Jack Adams. However, the evening before the bout was due to take place Ward was apprehended and bound over to keep the peace. The cancellation must have been a major disappointment to 'Young Molineaux' who, despite being much the smaller man and a considerable underdog, would have been confident of success. He subsequently showed his ability to triumph over bigger opponents by twice conquering the capable heavyweight William Renwick, although his most notable scalp was that of 'Hammer' Lane whom Wharton defeated in his final ring appearance.

Hibernians in a Murderous Mood

By the 1830s the number of deaths directly attributable to prize-fighting appears to have risen significantly. This could be, to some extent, a misleading impression due to greater coverage by the press of such tragedies. However, a more probable explanation is that, by then, the wealthy aristocratic patrons who had followed the Prince of Wales into the sport during the Mendoza era had largely withdrawn, leaving the financing to lower-order speculators who could ill afford to sustain any losses. These backers were likely to insist that boxers continued to struggle on when their cause was well and truly beyond redemption, an extremely dangerous practice which could not fail to jeopardize lives. It was at this time, although not for this reason, that Whetstone's only recorded death as a result of a regular pitched battle occurred.

The mill, a minor one for a purse of £5, took place on Tuesday 9 July 1833 in a field a short distance from the Green Man. It involved two bruisers who had both fought in the village before, namely Mike Murphy and the 'Paddington Pet', Ned Thompson. There was little hint at the start that the affair would degenerate into a violent tumult, but once Thompson demonstrated that he was the stronger man the unrest began. After three or four rounds a mob of Irishmen, realizing that their favourite was losing the bout, rioted in a most barbaric manner. Everyone within their reach was attacked with a variety of weapons including large sticks, bludgeons and whips. Even though the constable of Whetstone, Mr Touchbury, was present, he was powerless to intervene and watched helplessly as bystanders were knocked down and viciously assaulted. Amid much confusion the contest continued. A bottle was thrown as Thompson was falling, and sticks were placed for him to trip over, but the Paddington fighter kept his composure and persevered in the face of an increasingly perilous situation.

After about 45 minutes Murphy, whilst sitting on the knee of his second, Tom Reidie, declared that he did not wish to carry on. However, Murphy's brother Ned refused to give in for him and the two men dragged their charge once more to the mark. The conflict was therefore renewed, although because of the general mêlée it was impossible for the action to be seen clearly, and for the last couple of rounds at least the combatants were totally obscured from view. Eventually, so *The Times* reported, Thompson "received a tremendous blow on the head, from the effects of which he fell back and never rose again". He was conveyed to the house of a nearby surgeon, Mr John Harrison, where four pints of blood were taken and six leeches applied to his temple. Not surprisingly this expert medical aid failed to bring about the boxer's recovery. He was later removed to the Green Man where he continued to receive the attention of Mr Harrison and also a Mr Evans, assistant to another surgeon. He died at one o'clock on the Thursday morning.

The inquest was held the following day at the Green Man before Thomas Stirling and attracted great interest since an account had been circulated attributing Thompson's death to the brutal conduct of his opponent's supporters. Statements given by several witnesses left little doubt that he had been violently assaulted by the Irish mob, who were heard to say that they were determined their countryman should win at any cost. Frederick Tomkins, a carman from Paddington, described how bludgeons were going in all directions and the deceased was frequently hit. George Lord, a farrier from the same area, attested that he saw a man strike Thompson twice with a large stick. Mr Harrison was of the opinion that death was due to the "rupture of a blood-vessel on the brain, which might have proceeded from a fall, or a blow, or some other violent concussion". In answer to a question from the foreman, he asserted that the amount of blood taken from the patient was not excessive for a person in his condition.

The inquest was resumed on the Saturday with further depositions corroborating the earlier evidence. Although one Michael Mullaney insisted that the fight had been fair, his testimony was disregarded since two witnesses swore he had perpetrated an attack on Thompson. Mullaney was therefore swiftly taken into custody and committed to Newgate Prison. After one hour's deliberation the jury first made the point of calling the "attention of the proper authorities to the frequency of these disgusting occurrences (prize fights) in the neighbourhood". A verdict of manslaughter was then returned against nine men including the Murphy brothers, Tom Reidie and the just detained Mullaney.

On 9 September, at the Old Bailey, Tom Reidie was convicted of manslaughter but given a lenient gaol sentence of two months without hard labour as it was clear that he had not been involved in the mass affray. Strangely, Michael Mullaney, who had apparently been part of the lawless mob, was acquitted. The following month Mike Murphy was indicted for the wilful murder of his late opponent. Owing to his poor state of health (he was at the time in the last stages of consumption) the court ordered that he be discharged. He did not survive for long afterwards and the *Weekly Dispatch* of 17 November reported his demise during the previous week, as well as the arrest of Ned Murphy who was apprehended after having travelled from Ireland to attend his brother's funeral.

The prosecution of the elder Murphy, on 29 November, was the last to arise out of the case. It resulted in the prisoner, described in court as a 28-year old plasterer, being cleared of the charge of murder, the evidence against him having been found to be of a rather contradictory nature. The jury did, however, return a verdict of manslaughter, and six days later he was also sentenced to two months' imprisonment.

Sutton Wards off Future Champion

Nick Ward, brother of the celebrated champion Jem, was a pugilist of considerable potential who, owing to his lack of heart, proved a great disappointment to the Fancy. Although it is true that he did follow in the title-winning footsteps of his illustrious sibling, his championship win was most fortuitous and his ring performances generally poor.

In February 1835 Ward trained at the Five Bells public house in preparation for his début against ex-dragoon Harry Lockeyer. He made a winning start to his lack-lustre career but soon afterwards was bound over to keep the peace for 12 months. His return, on 27 May 1836, was a hastily arranged encounter for £5 and a purse, fixed up as a finale to the day's principal sport of cock-fighting. It was intended as a trial in which Ward could get his hand in before moving on to bigger and better things but, as will be seen, the affair instead offered the first evidence that Nick lacked the requisite fortitude of his elder brother.

The venue selected was a secluded paddock near Finchley owned by a gentleman farmer who had been amongst the aristocratic crowd assembled for the earlier entertainment. Ward's opponent, a black boxer called 'Sambo' Sutton, was an extraordinary character possessing the unusual gift of being able to dance, sing and drink while standing on his head. He was a man of great bodily strength and had shown some ability in sparring sessions, but was not expected to trouble the favourite unduly.

At seven o'clock in the evening the fighters set to under the critical eye of some of the best-known sportsmen in the country. Present were such renowned ring greats as John Gully, Tom Cribb, Tom Spring, Jem Ward and Peter Crawley, all champions of England in their time, as well as Tom Belcher, Dick Curtis and 'Young Dutch Sam', former heroes among the lighter men. They saw Ward begin the contest in promising fashion, scoring effectively to the head of his opponent and displaying good defensive skills whenever Sutton attempted to retaliate. In the third round the future champion drew first blood and he continued to control the bout until the 11th. At this point Sutton succeeded in drawing blood from Ward's nose, a feat he managed to repeat in the following round, although more by luck than good judgment. To the utter astonishment and, indeed, contempt of the distinguished audience, Ward then declared that he no longer wished to fight. Sutton was therefore proclaimed the surprise winner. The latter promptly demonstrated his diverse talents by standing on his head and singing a celebratory song whilst the loser hurried from the ground in disgrace.

Sutton's later career was not a great success, but he flourished as an instructor of self-defence and taught at the universities of both Oxford and Cambridge. In addition he made use of his theatrical aptitude and, according to his obituary in *Bell's Life in London*, "appeared as Othello and other characters at Liverpool, Marylebone Theatre and elsewhere". It is interesting to note that he, like Ward, also trained at the Five Bells. He was sent there by Jem Burn in October 1842 in preparation for his forthcoming meeting with an Australian named Gorrick, usually known as 'Bungaree'. (The next year he was again at Finchley to train for a

In addition to the Setting to, Sambo Sutton will perform

HIS ASTONISHING FEATS!

Dancing a Hornpipe on his Head,

And Sparring with his Feet while in that position.

The Setting-to will represent Shakspeare's Tragedy of

OTHELLO.

Iago............**DEAF BURKE**——Othello..........**SAMBO SUTTON**
Cassio...**JACK FORSIE**

The other Characters by Amateurs.

AFTER WHICH,

DEAF BURKE

WILL GIVE HIS CELEBRATED

Grecian Statues

For which he was so highly patronized in the United States.

In the course of the Evening,

SAMBO SUTTON

WILL SING

Such a Gettin up Stairs

AND

JUMP JIM CROW,

As sung by him at the London Theatres with great success.

Doors to be Opened at Seven o'clock, to Commence precisely at Half past.
Admission to the Stage 2s. 6d. Boxes 1s. 6d. Pit 1s. Gal. 6d.

PRIVATE LESSONS

Given by Sutton at the Humber-Tavern, Humber-street, daily, from
three to five, where tickets for the Benefit may also be had.

PECK, PRINTER, LOWGATE, HULL.

*17. Part of a poster advertising 'Sambo' Sutton's appearance at the Adelphi
Theatre, Hull, on 28 October 1839, during which the pugilist demonstrated
his unusual talents.
(Reproduced by kind permission of Michael Jones.)*

proposed bout with Harry Preston, for which he received forfeit when the latter's backer deserted him.) As for Ward himself, following a prevented rematch with Sutton and an unimpressive victory over Jem Bailey, he was manoeuvred into the title picture with a win over the veteran 'Deaf' Burke. In February 1841 a foul blow by an impetuous Ben Caunt gifted him the championship, but three months afterwards he capitulated meekly to the same fighter and immediately retired. He then pursued the customary occupations of publican and teacher of the noble art until his early demise on 17 February 1850 from an "affection of the lungs of long standing".

Bailey Butchered by Poulterer

On Tuesday 14 March 1837 yet another fighting butcher, by the name of Bailey, took on a young chicken-choker in a minor bout arranged for £5 a side. Both men were in business in the now defunct Newgate Market. (This was situated halfway between the prison of the same name and St Paul's Cathedral, in close proximity to what was, at the time, the most famous execution site in London.) The obscure match, which was set up by two salesman, took place in an open ring at Whetstone. It attracted little interest except, as *Bell's Life in London* quaintly put it, "among the 'keg-meg' purveyors who bestrode their 'living cat's-meat' in great puff and, as they 'bowled' along the road, looked 'who but me'".

Bailey was the son of the Smithfield butcher who had twice met Isaac Dobell. Like his unsuccessful father, he found the experience of fighting at Whetstone an unhappy one and was easily overcome by his superior opponent in a poor contest, the duration of which was not recorded.

Double Début

On 6 June 1837 two men made their débuts who were destined to become familiar figures within the sporting world, Johnny (Jack) Hannan and Dan Dismore. Whilst the former went on to make his mark as a noted fighter, his antagonist earned considerable respect as a backer and patron to those aspiring to fistic fame. At the time of their contest Dismore, a waiter and barman, was 25 years old, an age considered rather advanced for a first attempt in the prize-ring. Hannan, another battler to come out of the tough St Giles area, had youth on his side, being six years younger than his well-supported opponent.

The bout was scheduled for Colney Heath and *Bell's Life in London* reported that the toll collectors at the Whetstone-gate did brisk business as an animated mob flocked towards the venue. Payment was, in fact, not necessary there since the toll paid at the first gate out of London also covered Whetstone. However, many were unaware of this and the pikemen, to their great glee, were able to extract further monies. The crowd halted for their customary refreshments at the Green Dragon near Barnet, the training quarters of Dismore. Eventually a party, including the two fighters, set out towards Colney Heath. On arriving at the "White Hart, Mimms", it was intercepted by a returning Tom Oliver who had been prevented by magistrates from reaching the planned destination. A council of war opted for a retreat back to the Green Dragon; the group was followed by one of the 'beaks' who, on being persuaded that no hostilities would take place, rode off towards Barnet. He really should have been less naïve for, the moment he disappeared, an immediate move was made to Cockfosters where *Bell's Life* described a ring being formed "on a beautifully romantic spot at the commencement of Hadley Common".

Two battered-looking men, one with his arm in a sling, caused a considerable stir as they approached the roped area. They were the ubiquitous Owen Swift and Izzy Lazarus. The latter, a fine Jewish lightweight, had trained Dismore and would later emigrate to the United States where his 'grogshop' in Buffalo became a popular fight headquarters. Only five days previously the pair had fought a marathon 2 hour 15 minute battle and were now at ringside to officiate as umpires. The encounter began at a quarter past two, with Hannan drawing first blood in the very opening round. He continued to control the action through to the completion of the contest, for although the older fighter displayed remarkable bravery, he lacked the skill to retaliate effectively. By the 23rd and last round Dismore had sustained fearful punishment and there was little surprise when, after 1 hour 2 minutes, Jack Tisdale and Byng Stocks were forced to withdraw their charge. He was conveyed to his carriage and, extremely faint, taken away to be put to bed. Doubts were initially entertained regarding his chances of recovery, but fortunately these were unfounded.

The bitterly disappointed loser, realizing that he was too old to become a success in the prize-ring, opted to retire and change his calling to that of a publican. His enthusiasm for the sport never diminished and, in later years, the celebrated Bill Hayes was one of several pugilists who had cause to be grateful for Dismore's patronage. Hannan, meanwhile, having shown that he had the potential to become a first-rank boxer, would renew his association with the area on three further occasions.

Unhappy Day for the Prize-Ring Commissary

The bout at Colney Heath, on 17 October 1837, between Patsy M'Nolty and Naylor Murray, both competent but decidedly mediocre bruisers, was interrupted by two St Albans magistrates who imposed their authority and ordered the battle to cease. The suspended contest was therefore transferred to Cockfosters, and whilst the ring was being reassembled the protagonists rested in separate rooms at the nearby Stag Inn. The *Licensed Victuallers' Gazette*, writing about the event some fifty years later, detailed how the men were looked after during the enforced interval. According to this source M'Nolty was revived with "half a bottle of sherry with four eggs beaten up in it" and his opponent was sustained with "a cup of tea laced with brandy". Such measures might seem slightly unusual today, but at the time they were considered fairly commonplace. Indeed Daniel Mendoza, in his 1790 treatise *The Modern Art of Boxing*, suggested drinking half a pint of red wine mulled with brandy on the morning of an event and having available a "drink made of Holland's bitters, fine China orange juice, with some lump sugar" to be imbibed between rounds. Although Murray and M'Nolty apparently felt themselves to be much invigorated by the refreshments lavished upon them, the resumed bout did not last long. During the 15 rounds fought at the original venue, Murray had taken a decided lead and, after dominating a further six at Cockfosters, he was proclaimed the winner.

A second mill between Young Crawley and the rather unflatteringly named 'Pimple Bill' had hardly begun when the motley crowd present were charged by a mounted horse patrol armed with pistols and sabres. Under such circumstances they could hardly be blamed for frantically dispersing, leaving the hapless commissary Tom Oliver and his deputy Jack Clarke to face the brunt of the attack. Both men were rounded up and taken to Totteridge where the magistrate hearing the case decided that the alleged breach of peace did not come within his jurisdiction. They were subsequently transported to Hendon and brought before a clerical justice of the quorum. He ordered them to pay a surety of £20 each and to defray the expenses of the police which were calculated to be 35 shillings. In his capacity as commissary in charge of the prize-ring's ropes and stakes, Oliver was accustomed to the frequent difficulties generated by his duties. However, on days such as this, he must have yearned for the past when his problems had come in the more manageable shape of quality fighters such as Tom Shelton and George Cooper.

18. Tom Oliver, the diligent and respected commissary of the prize-ring.

Milling between the Classes

In November 1838 a curious confrontation highlighted the willingness with which gentlemen during the prize-ring era resorted to fisticuffs in order to settle their differences with the frequently aggressive proletariat. Such well-bred pugilistic exponents were often extremely competent, many having acquired their boxing skills in lessons with the leading fighters of the time. Of course this may not necessarily have been true of the Mr W involved in the particular altercation in question. However, since he had few difficulties when conceding weight to a significantly stronger antagonist, it can be assumed that he had been schooled at least moderately in the noble art.

The affair came about as a result of an incident which took place in a house near Golden Square, in the London district of Soho. Mr W, accompanied by a medical friend, had just entered the premises for the purpose of attending a concert when he was grossly insulted by a belligerent shoemaker. The presumptuous "cordwainer" then proceeded to challenge him to a fight for £5 and Mr W, despite being some two and a half stone the lighter, readily accepted. He promptly threw down his money but the cobbler was found to have only a sovereign and it was for this token sum that they agreed to do battle. The pair accordingly met at six o'clock the next morning and made their way by cabs to Finchley where, in a secluded spot between two haystacks, they squared up to one another.

It soon became evident to the shoemaker that he had made a grave error in initiating the confrontation. His 8-stone opponent may have given the appearance of an easy victim but the reality, from the point of view of the "big un", was disturbingly different. He suffered a painful and humiliating beating at the end of which, so *Bell's Life in London* eloquently recounted, the "cobbler's mug looked like a brewer's trotter covered with bunions".

Boxing Day Fiasco for Burn's Pupil

A little Christmas milling for the entertainment of the London sporting élite was appropriately arranged for Boxing Day in 1838. The location, in the same meadow near Finchley where Nick Ward and 'Sambo' Sutton had met two and a half years earlier, had been a closely guarded secret. As a result, attendance was restricted to not more than 150 spectators. Amongst these were many famous names from the boxing world, both past and present, including Tom Cribb, Tom Spring, 'Deaf' Burke, Tom Belcher, Dick Curtis, Barney Aaron and Johnny Hannan. The protagonists chosen to exhibit, a certain Jack Carter and a black pugilist named Kendrick, were both novices although the latter, at least, was not entirely unknown to the Fancy. No relation to the bruiser of the same name who had encountered George Cooper and Tom Oliver, he was one of Jem Burn's many pupils and had shown some prowess when performing at his mentor's sparring school. Carter, at around 10 stone, was conceding about a stone and a half in weight but, as a battler out of the notorious St Giles, he had no doubt found himself in more adverse situations.

As *Bell's Life in London* (30 December 1838) reported, "thirteen rounds were fought, in which the black proved himself a regular muff". The decisive point in the contest came in the fourth when Carter landed a heavy strike on Kendrick's right eye, which instantly swelled up so badly as to seriously impede his vision. From then on the bigger man put up an abject performance, his main aim appearing to be to prevent his confident opponent from inflicting any further damage. When Kendrick did make one final effort, he was caught with another crushing blow on the same eye which immediately brought about his prompt capitulation.

To be fair to Kendrick, some of his lack of fortitude could have been due to being unaccustomed to the climate – the cold, possibly, rather than Carter's punches, being responsible for sapping his will to fight. There was certainly a precedent for inclement weather adversely affecting a boxer unused to such conditions. It was believed, for instance, by Tom Molineaux's friends to be a major factor in the American's first defeat by Tom Cribb. (However, the challenger's determined showing on that occasion was indisputably of the highest order. Indeed Miles thought "a little manoeuvring" by Cribb's second may have had more to do with the final outcome.) Kendrick subsequently showed an improvement in a couple of further forays into the prize-ring, but it would not be accurate to describe his début as an especially auspicious one.

The Downfall of 'Deaf'

At this point James Burke re-enters the story for the final time. The intervening years had not been without incident. There was the notable win over Simon Byrne at No Mans Land in May 1833, which turned to tragedy with the death of the Irishman, and the frustration of fruitless attempts to get the champion, Jem Ward, to share a ring with him. When a match was not forthcoming, the 'Deaf'un' claimed the title and headed to America where, in New Orleans, he was forced to flee for his life from the marauding supporters of one of his opponents.

Burke's first contest back in England was against the artful Nottingham fighter William Thompson. Better known by the appellation of 'Bendigo', he was a rather wild eccentric who in his last years reformed and became a preacher. The occasion was scheduled for 12 February 1839, and gained added significance when Jem Ward agreed to present the victor with a champion's belt. No doubt due to Burke's recent trip, the affair provoked as much interest in the United States as it did on the home shores, and a major American sporting newspaper was inundated with requests for details to be published.

Accompanied by his faithful 'secretary' Tommy Roundhead, the 'Deaf'un' began his preparations in Brighton. He later switched his headquarters to Finchley since, according to *Bell's Life in London*, "he feared his devotion to the young Queen on her arrival at the Pavilion might have interfered with his training". However, if this comment gave the impression that Burke was wholly committed to reaching the peak of fitness, the truth was, in fact, very different. Always an obstinate man, he ignored the advice of those with his best interests at heart, being led astray by admirers whose dissipated habits were totally at variance with the disciplined way of life to which he should have been adhering. In addition, an old knee injury, which precluded extensive walking and running, did little to help his cause. During the bout, in Leicestershire, the full extent of his lack of conditioning became painfully apparent – sluggish and devoid of judgment, he absorbed considerable punishment before deliberately conceding the fight by twice butting 'Bendigo' in the 10th round.

'Bendigo' too suffered serious damage to his knee-cap whilst throwing a somersault in March 1840, and the field was then left open. However, a further loss, to Nick Ward in September, finally knocked Burke out of the championship reckoning. His experience at least enabled him to wind up his career on a winning note by subduing Bob Castles in 1 hour 10 minutes on 13 June 1843. He became a familiar sight around the less salubrious nightspots of the metropolis, playing the role of companion to gentlemen wishing to frequent such establishments. His early death from phthisis on 8 January 1845 was hardly surprising given his unhealthy later lifestyle, but, as Miles pointed out, "his good qualities were his own, his vices the grafting of his so-called 'betters' in society".

Hannan's Training Sojourns

In March 1839 the backers of Johnny Hannan, determined that he should be in prime condition for a second match with rising star Johnny Walker, sent their man to the Bald Faced Stag, Finchley, under the expert care of Harry Holt and Bob Fuller. Holt, nicknamed the 'Cicero of the Ring', was a respected figure within the sport. A former pugilist himself, he was nearly the equal of Dick Curtis and Tom Belcher as a second and was also an accomplished fistic reporter. His companion, Fuller, had built up a reputation as a champion pedestrian and was generally recognized as one of the finest trainers of prize-fighters in the country. As *Bell's Life in*

19. The versatile 'Cicero of the Ring', Harry Holt, pugilist, second, trainer and journalist.

London drolly commented, Hannan's "mawleys and trotters were alike under scientific guidance". Holt worked their charge with the gloves whilst Fuller took the boxer through a punishing schedule on the road. Hannan, for his part, was conscientious in his work and only once felt the need to go astray, this being after a visit by the irrepressible 'Deaf' Burke. Holt, though, was alert to the situation and the fighter found himself bundled off to his room where he was locked safely in to prevent further temptation. The efforts of all concerned paid off as, during the contest, Hannan was able to call on unexpected reserves of strength and emerge the victor after a prolonged battle of 3 hours and 48 minutes' duration.

The training regime having been successful last time out, Hannan returned to the Bald Faced Stag in May under the supervision of Holt to prepare for a bout against Byng Stocks. However, on this occasion his bigger opponent prevailed, Johnny going down to an eight-round defeat on 11 June at Royston Heath. He fared little better 19 months later when, following his last training excursion to the Barnet area, he succumbed in 79 minutes to the unbeaten Johnny Broome in a fight arranged for the substantial sum of £500 a side.

This proved to be Hannan's final ring appearance. He was appointed landlord of the Coach and Horses, St Martin's Lane, London (a popular sporting house which had a succession of pugilistic hosts) but failed dismally in business and thereafter scraped a living as an occasional teacher and second. *Bell's Life* of 25 October 1857 reported his death from consumption "brought on by his too great fondness for late hours and gay society" and added the tribute that "as a pugilist and teacher of his art, Jack Hannan stood in the very first rank".

20. *'The Royal Bruce Passing the Bald-Faced Stag, Finchley'.*
Engraving (c. 1830) after an original by James Pollard.

Police Outwitted

On 23 April 1839, Whetstone was selected as the site for a mill the next day between Robert Noon, a Drury Lane lad who had won a couple of minor skirmishes, and a tailor of more experience by the name of James Hood. Both men came from boxing backgrounds. Noon was the brother of the tragic 'Pocket Hercules' and Hood, the 'Chelsea Star', son of a fighting 'snip' best known for having participated in a turn-up with the invincible Jack Randall.

The forces of law and order being more vigilant than ever before, strict care was taken to keep the event as secret as possible. In addition, it was deemed advisable to schedule the fixture for an early hour. However, these precautions proved to be in vain for, by seven o'clock in the morning, the police had somehow been alerted and were primed to interfere. No sooner had Jack Clarke, on this occasion in charge of the ropes and stakes, led a procession of the Fancy out of London than they were joined by two constables in a cart, accompanied by a three-horse patrol. The unwelcome additions were diligent in their duties and tenaciously hung on to their quarry so, as they neared the planned destination, Clarke gave the command to abandon Whetstone and move on to Barnet. There the police officers attached themselves to the pugilists to prevent them from quietly disappearing and, since there was no point in forming a ring under such circumstances, Clarke ordered a retreat back to town.

On reaching Soho with the obstructive tail still in evidence, a lengthy discussion took place at a nearby public house and, after due deliberation, the office was given for Woolwich. Hood and Noon, heavily disguised, made their way to Westminster where a steamer had been chartered by 'Stunning' Joe Banks, an influential St Giles publican whose hostelry was a fashionable hangout for young bloods and members of both the boxing and underworld fraternities. Although the fighters managed to get on board undetected, Clarke was not so successful. Indeed, so closely did the police follow him that it proved impossible to smuggle the ropes and stakes on to any river boat in the immediate vicinity, and consequently they had to be left behind. Clarke himself took the officers on a pleasant little tour of Wimbledon Common whilst, in the meantime, a suitable field was located about halfway between Woolwich and Greenwich where the contest could go ahead unimpeded.

When a few men had been positioned at various intervals around a 30-foot spot, the battle finally commenced amidst great rejoicing from the patient, and by then well-travelled, spectators. Noon drew first blood and also scored the first knock-down in the process of eventually overcoming the tailor in a fair and sporting encounter lasting one and three quarter hours. To the watching crowd the winner's stopping ability may have evoked, with a little bit of imagination, memories of his late brother, but his hitting could only have been described as poor. Noon, nevertheless, was so delighted with his success that he celebrated by running 200 yards before jumping a water ditch some seven feet wide.

PART III - THE LATTER TIMES

*I should be sorry to see prizefighting go out.
Every art should be preserved, and the art of self-
defence is surely important ... prizefighting makes people
unaccustomed not to be alarmed at seeing their own
blood or feeling a little pain from a wound.*

Dr Samuel Johnson

Poisoned at the Five Bells?

The celebrated Bloomsbury lightweight Tom Maley, credited by *Bell's Life in London* with fighting "some of the longest and determined battles on record", took his 'breathings' at the Five Bells on three separate occasions during a lengthy and meritorious career. His first visit occurred in the summer of 1836 when he trained at the Finchley public house prior to an unsuccessful encounter with Izzy Lazarus at Colney Heath. Two years later, under the auspices of Jack Clarke, he returned to the Five Bells to prepare for his contest with the up-and-coming Johnny Hannan; on 30 August 1838 he secured an undeserved 11th-round victory after his St Giles opponent was adjudged to have delivered a foul blow.

When Maley was matched for the first of four bouts with the Nottingham veteran Sam Merryman, to take place on 23 June 1840,

21. The Five Bells, Finchley (c.1900), still recognisable as the training headquarters favoured by prize-fighters over half a century earlier.
(Reproduced by kind permission of Barnet Local Studies and Archives.)

Peter Crawley decided the tried and tested Five Bells would be an excellent training venue for his protégé who, on this occasion, was backed by persons of considerable influence. No expense was spared in the attempt to bring the 'Bloomsbury Pet' to peak fitness, and Jack Clarke was again appointed to oversee his conditioning regime. However, after ten days of hard work under the watchful eye of his respected trainer, Maley suddenly began suffering from agonising pains in his stomach and loins, accompanied by frequent diarrhoea and vomiting. The opinion of the doctor attending the fighter was that the symptoms were caused by his having digested some poisonous substance. This diagnosis understandably alarmed Clarke who was certain that someone had undertaken to 'nobble' his charge. Crawley was urgently summoned but disagreed that foul play was responsible for Maley's severely weakened condition, although he did concur with Clarke's request for an immediate evacuation of the quarters.

Once moved to new surroundings (Norwood), Maley made a good recovery and was able to fit in three weeks of satisfactory preparation before the day of the meeting. Whether or not the poisoning was accidental or deliberate was never ascertained. If it was the latter, the attempt was manifestly a failure since Maley's strength was unimpaired throughout the 2 hour 1 minute contest. At the onset Merryman was the better boxer but, following a cross-buttock throw in the 11th round, the tide of battle changed in favour of the lighter man who demonstrated once again that "youth will be served".

Prodigy Fails to Fulfil Potential

By the time Ned Adams went to train at Finchley in July 1840 he was, at the age of 17, well versed in the fistic art. This is scarcely surprising since he was related to the acclaimed Jack Adams, whom he ably assisted when the latter established himself as a teacher in Paris. (Definitely coming from fighting stock, Ned was reported by

Bell's Life in London to be Jack's brother, whilst much later, *Famous Fights Past and Present* was adamant that theirs was a nephew / uncle relationship.) After two victories in France, Ned returned to England where, in March 1840, he beat Tom Smith; four months later he was to be found at the Five Bells preparing for an encounter with Jack Forsey. As has been seen, the Five Bells was a favourite haunt for training purposes during this period and, according to an entry in the diaries of Eliza Anne Salvin (daughter of the architect, Anthony Salvin), it was even the venue for the occasional, albeit unchronicled, prize-fight. There Adams was taken in hand by the experienced duo of "the elder Jack" and the respected pedestrian, Bob Fuller. The contest itself took place at Horsell, near Woking, on 21 July and resulted in a victory for the youngster after a marathon 2 hour 25 minute battle.

Adams was back at Finchley in the autumn of the same year to train for his October match with the aforementioned Tom Maley. Again Bob Fuller was responsible for putting him through his paces and, on the day, he chalked up the fifth win of his unbeaten career, overcoming the 'Bloomsbury Pet' in 64 rounds near Royston.

In January 1841 Ned returned to the Five Bells in preparation for his next fight, against Dick Cain of Leicester. The young prodigy was by this time so highly regarded that Cain's backers, despite their man's competent past performances, refused to put money on him until they were given highly favourable odds. The over-confident Adams was not as conscientious as he should have been in the build-up to the bout. Consequently he suffered his first defeat when the two met in Bedfordshire on 9 February. He never did fulfil the immense promise of his youth and two years afterwards bid farewell to an active boxing career.

There is little doubt that Adams would have become one of the prize-ring's great lightweights had he been more carefully nurtured in his formative years. He did, however, make a significant contribution to the sport in that, in later life, he was instrumental in the founding of the Pugilistic Benevolent Association (set up principally to assist pugilists in need of help and to keep order during contests). An indication of the respect in which he was held is demonstrated by a poem especially composed by Renton Nicholson to advertise a benefit for Adams, held on 18 October 1852 at Saville House in Leicester Square:

Ned's bravery and truth were never doubted;
He fought till deaf to time, when time was shouted;
Thus gaining in defeat respect and fame,
Which never grace the knave or coward's name.
In victory calm, no bounce to dim his laurels,
In temper good, and excellent in morals;
Such is Ned Adams, and a boxer rare.
Uphold him on the night in Leicester-square.
Shell out your bobs; or, if his care you'd drown,
For luck's sake, handicap him with a crown.

Adams died in poverty at the age of 39 on 17 June 1862 at his lodgings in Charlotte Street, London. He was buried the following week at the St Marylebone Cemetery, Finchley. A short distance from Ned's former training headquarters, the Five Bells, this burial ground had been established some eight years previously on a site described by *The Builder* as a "retired and rural spot". Adams's interment is registered in the cemetery records under his real name of Edward Morgan and he is listed as being inhumed in public grave no. K12/98.

Larcenous Goings-on

Whilst Whetstone played host to many respected and indeed respectable boxers, it equally proved a mecca for the unprincipled elements who allied themselves to the sport. The *Weekly Dispatch* of 20 April 1834 deplored the prevalence of regular mills in the village "got up exclusively by thieves" with little or no connection to the recognized prize-ring. The paper further cited an instance where those involved in such an occurrence "surrounded a baker's shop, broke it open, and plundered him of every particle of bread on the premises" causing "the inhabitants [to] shut up their houses in terror". It was not until the summer of 1842, however, that a pugilist himself was to be guilty of larcenous conduct in the neighbourhood.

At the end of July of that year Reuben Marten, now 42 years old, commenced training at Whetstone for his forthcoming match against 'Bungaree'. Although he was looked after by Tom Callas and later joined by Dick Curtis, who was to be one of his seconds, Marten's commitment to the task in hand soon began to appear suspect. On Saturday 6 August, Tom Spring, returning from an outing to see his old friend Tom Belcher, spotted the fighter in the Bald Faced Stag at Finchley in the company of three very unsavoury characters. The next day Marten assured friends who visited him that he was in excellent shape and ready for action. However, during the contest on the Tuesday, he did not even attempt to throw a single punch in a disgraceful affair that lasted just four and a half minutes. If this blatant dishonesty was far from satisfactory, even to those members of the Fancy hardened by the increasing frequency of such behaviour, what subsequently came to light did little to enhance the sport's already tarnished reputation.

Bell's Life in London (21 August 1842) described in detail all of Marten's transgressions. It seems that from the moment he left London to begin 'training', he was determined to defraud as many tradesman as possible, not only in Whetstone but further afield in Barnet and Potters Bar. These he referred for payment to his backers, who had never undertaken to meet the large bills he ran up. He also borrowed money on several occasions from the landlord of the Green Man where he was staying, whilst having absolutely no intention of settling this debt. Even Marten's seconds were not immune to his deceit since he made their remuneration subject to his winning, fully knowing that he was about to perpetrate a 'cross'. (They, at least, did not remain completely out of pocket as, later in the month, a subscription was made on their behalf at Spring's Castle Tavern.)

Surprisingly, given Marten's unscrupulous tendencies, he does not appear to have joined the disreputable band of bruisers who found themselves transported to New South Wales. He was, however, a regular visitor to the Insolvent Debtors' Court and, like so many of his profession, ended his days in straitened circumstances.

Demise at Barnet

On Sunday 28 August 1842, *Bell's Life in London* notified its readers of the "death of Harry Harmer, one of the old school, which took place on Sunday last at Barnet". Harmer, although not as well known as his famed cousins the Belcher brothers, was nevertheless an extremely competent and scientific boxer who was unfortunate enough to have his career curtailed by a severe opthalmic condition. A coppersmith, he was one of a select body of prize-fighters to retire undefeated. Shortly after his last victory, over Tom Shelton, he sparred on a stage erected on a race-course near Montmartre (France) in front of an audience which included the Duke of Wellington. Harmer married the Belchers' sister Mary and, like his brother-in-law, Tom, was another of the milling fraternity chosen to keep order at the coronation of King George IV. Egan described him as a well-behaved inoffensive man and he was apparently much respected by the Fancy.

Following the untimely end to his fighting activities, Harmer became the landlord of the Plough in Smithfield, and on retiring from this second calling moved to a property in Barnet. The June 1841 census returns for the area show him to be of independent means and residing with his wife in Trafalgar Place, West Lane

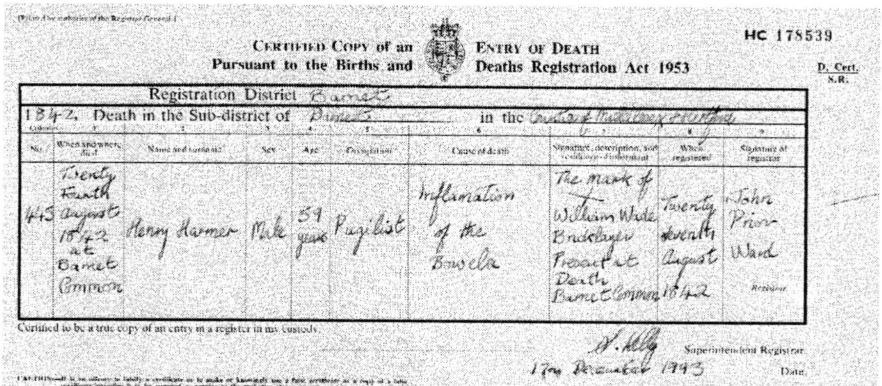

HC 178539

CERTIFIED COPY of an ENTRY OF DEATH
Pursuant to the Births and Deaths Registration Act 1953

D. Cert.
S.R.

Registration District Barnet

1842. Death in the Sub-district of Barnet in the

No.	When and where died	Name and surname	Sex	Age	Occupation	Cause of death	Signature, description, and residence of informant	When registered	Signature of registrar
445	Twenty Fourth August 1842 at Barnet Common	Henry Harmer	Male	59 years	Pugilist	Inflamation of the Bowels	The mark of William White Bricklayer Present at Death Barnet Common	Twenty seventh August 1842	John Prior Ward Registrar

Certified to be a true copy of an entry in a register in my custody.

Superintendent Registrar.

17th December 1993 Date.

22. A copy of the death certificate of Harry Harmer,
one of the eighteen pugilistic bodyguards employed at the coronation of George IV.
(The design of the death certificate is Crown copyright and is reproduced with the kind permission of the Controller of HMSO.)

(later West End Lane), not far from the Barnet Union Workhouse. He was listed as living next door to a William Wade, beer-seller, whose premises appear to have become subsequently the Lord Nelson public house.

While Miles, in *Pugilistica,* stated that the demise of Harmer occurred in 1834, and *Bell's Life* recorded the date as being 21 August 1842, it appears that both these sources are in error, though *Bell's Life* is much closer to the mark. According to the pugilist's death certificate, the event actually took place on Wednesday 24 August 1842 when, aged 59, he expired on Barnet Common from "inflamation [*sic*] of the bowels".

Hail the 'American Giant'

The tallest bareknuckle fighter to perform on British soil was a native of Michigan by the name of Charles Freeman, often referred to in contemporary newspapers as the 'American Giant'. Ben Caunt, the then champion of England, discovered Freeman during his visit to the United States and brought his protégé back home with him when he returned in March 1842. *Bell's Life in London*, on the 13th of that month, reported the arrival of both men at Liverpool and stated that the American "stands 7 feet 3 inches and is proportioned accordingly". The paper later decided this to be a slight exaggeration and, in October, amended its estimation to not quite seven feet in height. Two months later Freeman was measured at Regent's Park Barracks and found to be actually 6 feet 9 inches by the regimental standard. This was still an astounding size for the time and, not surprisingly, he elicited considerable awe from the packed crowds he drew during his exhibition tour of the country with Caunt.

At the end of September 1842, the 'Tipton Slasher', William Perry, was named as the opponent for Freeman's ring début. The following month Caunt took his charge to train at the Duke of York, Ganwick Corner, near Barnet, which was under the auspices of Frank Keys, a friend of the champion. The retired Bow Street officer soon had cause to regret this acquaintanceship for the giant was not an easy guest.

Besides the immense difficulty of his sleeping accommodation, there was also the problem of catering for the vast quantities of food needed to sustain his massive frame. The first dilemma was solved by placing two bedsteads foot to foot while Mr Keys manfully overcame the latter, although privately fearing the prospect of a famine.

Freeman resided for seven weeks at the Duke of York and applied himself diligently to the gruelling routine organized by Caunt. This consisted for the most part of 20- to 30-mile walks,

23. Charles Freeman, the tallest man to appear in an English bareknuckle contest.

during which he was frequently followed by groups of gawping locals. Much of his conditioning was undertaken in Squire Byng's park, the owner being a keen sportsman who generously placed his land at the fighter's disposal. In addition to his pedestrian activities, the American also performed dumb-bell exercises to increase his already prodigious strength. This practice in pugilistic preparation had originally been introduced by Tom Owen, whose achievements as a teacher almost matched those of his former victim, Daniel Mendoza.

The effectiveness of Freeman's training regime can be gauged by the fact that, despite his enormous appetite, he managed to rid himself of approximately five stone of unwanted weight. Consequently, when stripped for battle on 6 December 1842, he presented one of the most formidable sights ever witnessed within the prize-ring. Unfortunately, like other giants who have attempted to find fistic fame through the years, Freeman's boxing ability did not quite match up to his imposing physical appearance. He eventually succeeded in defeating Perry at the third attempt, after their first encounter had been interrupted and the second prevented, but never fought again, preferring instead to concentrate on stage performances. Less than three years later he died, far from home, a victim of consumption brought on by careless living. Despite some American press interest in Freeman's overseas pugilistic exploits, notably in the *Spirit of the Times*, he remained largely unknown to his fellow countrymen. However, John Carmel Heenan, when in England to meet Tom Sayers in the Great International Prize-Fight, paid a personal tribute to the memory of the Michigan colossus by erecting a monument at his own expense in West Hill Cemetery, Winchester, where Freeman was buried.

As for Ben Caunt, Freeman's English mentor, it may well have been he who was commemorated when the Great Bell of Westminster was given the appellation 'Big Ben'. Although the bell is generally believed to have been named after Sir Benjamin Hall, the then commissioner of works, there is a theory that it was the powerful prize-fighter who was thus honoured.

24. *Ben Caunt, who was responsible for bringing the 'American Giant' to England.*

Failed Conspiracy

The Jem Knowlton (Noulton)–Peter Stevens fiasco of October 1844 was, as *Bell's Life in London* so scathingly commented, "bottomed in fraud" from the start. Both men involved in the shabby affair had achieved little recognition in the prize-ring although Knowlton could at least boast an unbeaten record. After successfully contesting several bye-battles in Islington's Copenhagen Fields, he had made his début on 27 April 1842, cleverly defeating one Nat Griffin in 66 minutes. He first became acquainted with Finchley in February of the next year when, having notched up a further two wins over a pugilistic nonentity by the name of Anthony Burt, he went to train there for a forthcoming mill with Jack Greenstreet. On this occasion he was guilty of no more than poor preparation, being, on the day before the fight, still three pounds over the agreed 9 stone 9 pound limit. His lack of conditioning left Knowlton panting almost from the off and forced him to keep his mouth open "as if the fly-catching season had already commenced". However, he still managed to emerge victorious after a mediocre bout.

Knowlton's next contest, a 45-minute win over 'Oxford Charley' in March 1844, saw him seconded by a certain Peter Stevens. A native of Camden Town, Stevens had shown a reasonable level of commitment and determination up to that point in his career. This was in complete contrast to the dishonourable behaviour he would demonstrate from then on. During September 1844, Knowlton and Stevens met at The Grapes, a Clerkenwell public house run by Jack Tisdale, and a fight was arranged between the two to take place on the 22nd of the following month. Knowlton returned to Finchley to prepare but, 48 hours before the date in question, his proposed rival was seen close to his training quarters, often an indication that the impending hostilities were likely to be tarnished by chicanery.

The encounter between Bob Caunt, brother of Ben, and Nobby Clarke having terminated in favour of the latter, the assembled crowd gathered on the Kentish coast marshes were denied further entertainment when Stevens refused to enter the ring. He claimed he had made the match under the impression that Knowlton was to weigh no more than 9 stone 8 pounds whereas his opponent was now scaling considerably more. Although admitting that, since he could not read, he was unsure whether the confinement clause had been included in the articles drawn up, he nevertheless could not be persuaded to change his mind.

It did not come as a great shock to the Fancy when the weight limitation excuse subsequently proved to have been concocted by Stevens to hide his reason for declining to do battle. The truth of the matter was that the two bruisers, along with Stevens's backer, had organized the bout with the decided aim of swindling some wealthy Oxford supporters of Knowlton. Their plans, however, were dealt an irretrievable setback when Knowlton failed to obtain any money from this source and was thus obliged to seek recourse from his London friends. Since defrauding these was not his intention, he was forced to inform his fellow conspirators that the previously agreed 'cross' was no longer acceptable. Stevens, knowing that he had little chance against a superior adversary who was fighting to win, therefore resorted to the said course of action to avoid what would, almost certainly, have been a rather painful defeat.

He may not have profited from the Knowlton affair but there can be little doubt that Stevens did reap some financial remuneration from his next and final sortie into the prize-ring. On that occasion he dominated his bout with Charley George until, presumably having received his instructions, he declined to continue. This so disgusted his seconds that they resorted to kicking him whilst the referee was of the opinion that he ought to have been ducked in a nearby pond. *Bell's Life* merely commented that "knowing the conduct of Stevens in his match with Knowlton we are only surprised that anyone placed confidence in his honesty". Knowlton himself returned to the sport just one more time when in March 1851, as an out of condition 36-year-old, he met a Borough man called Tom Fury in a grudge encounter that was terminated by darkness.

Dover Champion Billeted at Whetstone

The navvies, bricklayers and miners employed to build the nation's railway system were, in the main, a particularly belligerent group. They took considerable pleasure in spoiling for trouble and were given to indulging in frequent brutal fights amongst themselves. Owing to the physical nature of their work, and the belief that to carry out their tasks adequately they had to be extremely well fed, they were generally brawny, tough individuals capable of inflicting considerable damage with their fists. According to *Gale's Licensed Victuallers' Mirror,* a huge gang of these labourers was at one period billeted at Whetstone whilst working on laying the line for the Great Northern Railway. Amongst this contingent was a bricklayer by the name of Bob Wade, a native of Derby, who had acquired the title of Dover champion some years previously when engaged by the Southern Eastern Railway on the London-to-Dover line.

Throughout his stay at Whetstone, Wade apparently asserted his authority over all but one of his fellow workers game enough to challenge his milling supremacy. The exception was Richard Frazer, a hardy miner weighing over 13 stone, with whom Wade fought three or four 'friendly' contests. As is the case with many such skirmishes between men involved in railway construction, scant information on their encounters exists. However, it is known that in all his attempts the Dover champion was unable to establish any superiority over his robust rival. At length Peter Crawley, believing that a regular match between the two would provide excellent entertainment for his patrons, arranged for them to meet for £10 a side, near Edenbridge in Kent, on 14 May 1850. Wade was the favourite and appeared to be gaining the advantage in a gruelling fight when, in the 33rd round, he fell victim to the strength of Frazer's powerful right hand.

Not long after this defeat, Wade was given the opportunity of retrieving his laurels in a contest with Aaron Jones, at the time a promising young protégé of Jem Burn. Despite a brave effort, however, he was again vanquished and, since the victor failed to win any of his remaining bouts (admittedly against first-class men), Wade had the dubious distinction of providing Jones with his only pugilistic success. Perhaps a better claim to fame should be that he is believed to have encouraged the young Tom Sayers in the sport. In fact the future champion most likely seconded Wade in one or two of his impromptu battles during the period they worked together on the Brighton and Lewes Railway. The former would later avenge Wade's loss at the hands of Jones on the way to establishing his reputation as one of the prize-ring's true immortals.

Tom Sayers and the 'Benicia Boy'

Tom Sayers was probably the most remarkable of the bareknuckle champions to visit the Barnet area. Standing but 5 feet 8 ½ inches tall and with a fighting weight never exceeding 11 stone, he fought his way up from the lowest level of the middleweights to the pinnacle of fistic achievement. Born in May 1826, he was a bricklayer by trade and worked on the Preston viaduct (near Brighton) before moving to the capital where he obtained employment on the London and North-Western Railway. It was not until 19 March 1849, however, that he had his first recognized regular prize-ring bout, easily defeating one Aby C(r)ouch in under 13 minutes. (Undoubtedly, though, before this he was involved in some of the numerous minor mills and turn-ups which regularly took place wherever large numbers of construction workers congregated.)

By 1856, Sayers had notched up five victories with just one loss (to middleweight champion Nat Langham) and was looking to test himself against heavyweight opposition. A win in January of that year over Nottingham's Harry Poulson propelled him into the position of potential title contender and, after beating Aaron Jones 13 months later, he issued a challenge to William Perry who at the time was claiming the championship. Many felt that the doughty 'Tipton Slasher' would be too big for his ambitious opponent, but the veteran's abilities had diminished considerably. On 16 June 1857 Sayers adroitly triumphed over the lumbering Perry in a contest of ten rounds occupying 1 hour 42 minutes. He subsequently scored successes against the novice Bill Benjamin (twice), the experienced Tom Paddock and the popular Bob Brettle, but saved the greatest performance of his outstanding career until last.

The Great International Prize-Fight of 17 April 1860, at Farnborough, saw Sayers pitted against the self-styled champion of America, John C Heenan, in a clash that fired the public's imagination on both sides of the Atlantic. The 'Benicia Boy' was the first foreign challenger for the championship of England since Tom Molineaux nearly half a century earlier, and the occasion temporarily evoked memories of the sport's heyday. The battle more than lived up to pre-fight expectations as, for 2 hours 20 minutes, the men pounded each other remorselessly. Heenan showed the greater aggression, and damage to Sayers's principal weapon, his right arm, did little to help the Englishman's cause. However, the latter's well-placed punches left his opponent virtually blinded, and by the time the contest was terminated in the 42nd round, with the ring completely overrun, both boxers had been severely punished. The result was later declared a draw and, after some wrangling, it was agreed that a replica of the championship belt should be made and presented to each participant.

With the advent of the Great Northern Railway, Barnet Races had regained some of their old popularity, lost when the common lands had been enclosed. A big attraction at the 1860 meeting was the legendary boxer whose fame at this point had reached its zenith. Sayers was no stranger to Hertfordshire for, some 11 years previously, he had lived in the county whilst working on the viaduct being constructed at Digswell. It is more than possible, therefore, that he had visited Barnet, and particularly the races, prior to the year of the Heenan bout, but this cannot be verified. The 1860 meeting took place on the last day of Barnet Fair, 6 September. Two days later the *Barnet Gazette* reported that "the redoubtable champion, Tom Sayers, was a conspicuous object during the afternoon, as he rode up and down the course, ever and anon exchanging the charger on which he was mounted for a horse of a different color [*sic*]".

In recognition of Sayers upholding English pride in the Great International Prize-Fight, a substantial sum was raised by public subscription and invested to ensure that his future was comfortably provided for. Aware that the interest on this would only be paid on condition that he never fought again, Sayers prepared himself for a life away from the ring. Aiming to capitalize on his widespread popularity, he began exhibiting with Messrs Howes and Cushing's Great United States Circus and, in *Bell's Life in London* (13 October 1861), announced that he had taken over as its proprietor. He renamed his acquisition Champion Circus and by the following month was claiming that 300,000 people had visited his show since the change of management.

One of the towns to which Sayers took the circus during this initial period was Barnet. According to *Bell's Life* the date was originally to have been 12 November but, for reasons not given, the schedule was advanced by five days. Included in the mammoth entertainment were two demonstrations by the pugilist himself, in which he set to with his regular sparring partner, Young Brooks of Birmingham. Unfortunately, the *Barnet Gazette* did not see fit to report on this, even though it had alerted its readers to the event the previous week. B J Angle (the renowned referee who officiated at the John L Sullivan–Charlie Mitchell prize-fight) told in his autobiography of being taken to meet Sayers "when that redoubtable warrior visited Barnet with a travelling circus". Again no details were given, but the eight-year-old Angle was apparently extremely proud of shaking hands with his idol whom he described as being, at that time, the "hero of the hour".

Like many of his fellow fistic champions, Sayers's abilities as a businessman did not begin to compare with his talents within the ropes. His circus quickly foundered, and was sold off at Hendon in November 1862. There can be little doubt that the free-living existence the fighter enjoyed during his time as an itinerant showman took a significant toll on his health. He had failed to reach the age of 40 when, on 8 November 1865, he breathed his last at Camden Town. Sayers had been responsible for a brief resurgence

25. The Champion Circus of the immortal Tom Sayers

of interest in the declining prize-ring and it was apt that his funeral provided the last great gathering of the pugilistic multitude.

The other participant in the Great International Prize-Fight, John C Heenan, also had occasion to exhibit his sparring skills in the Barnet area. In *Bell's Life* (22 March 1863) Mr Howes, having returned to the world of the circus, notified the public that the 'Benicia Boy' would tour "for a short season previous to the forthcoming meeting with Tom King". At one stage Finchley was listed in the itinerary, but there seems to have been a change of plan with Barnet being substituted

26. John C Heenan,
Tom Sayers' American opponent in
the Great International Prize-Fight.

instead. The date of this appearance, advertised in the *Sporting Life* of the Saturday before, was Friday 15 May 1863. Heenan was accompanied by William Evans, known as 'Young Broome', a former victim of the American's next opponent. No description of the display exists but, from previous accounts of Heenan's exploits with the gloves, it may be assumed that, despite its friendly nature, 'Young Broome' would have been fortunate to have emerged totally unscathed.

Against King in December, Heenan failed to recapture the form he had shown at Farnborough and, although he initially did well, his third and last contest ended in defeat after 35 minutes. Like Tom Sayers, the 'Benicia Boy' also expired prematurely, dying in his manager's arms on 25 October 1873 whilst on the way to San Francisco.

Napper's Tale

George Crockett, a top-class lightweight at the veteran stage of his career, was responsible in June 1863 for introducing to the London milling aficionados a young cabinetmaker by the name of Edward Bilborough. The 18-year-old novice who, under the *nom de guerre* of Ted Napper would go on to achieve considerable fame, was backed from a public house in the Barbican. He was sent to train for his maiden outing, under the supervision of Crockett's brother, to the Mitre at Barnet. (This hostelry already had a tenuous link with the prize-ring since it is known to have been visited by the famous lexicographer Dr Samuel Johnson, who was a fervent advocate and, on occasion, practitioner of the fistic science.)

Napper's mentor obviously had a lot of faith in his pupil's ability for he lined up as his first opponent the tough Jack Hartley, a brave performer who had mixed with some of the leading lightweights of the day. Their meeting may have been Ted's début but he showed the poise of an experienced campaigner and, after a ferocious struggle occupying 61 minutes, succeeded in knocking Hartley out of time with a powerful right hand to the jaw. It was, declared the *Illustrated Sporting News and Theatrical Review* (20 June), "one of the gamest battles for two miniature boxers that we have seen for a long time", and it provided ample evidence that a major new talent had arrived on the scene.

The next engagement for Napper took place in October the same year when he fought a 3 hour 16 minute draw with Bob Furze, the more capable of two sturdy fighting siblings. (The younger suffered from a disfiguring squint and hence was known as 'Bos' Furze, which gave rise to a certain potential for confusion.) Napper was then matched at 8 stone 8 pounds with the clever Wolverhampton warrior Abe Hicken, the mill to come off on Tuesday 5 April 1864 for £25 a side. He was sent to the Five Bells to prepare in the company of his last opponent and, a fortnight before the day in question, Nap Lawley arrived to oversee proceedings. The latter was rather old-fashioned in his approach to training but he knew his job well and could be relied upon to bring his charges up to peak physical condition. Amongst others he had supervised was Tom King prior to that fighter's great effort against John C Heenan. Ted was a diligent worker, always ready to listen to advice, and under the disciplinarian Lawley he was soon in excellent shape and within the required weight.

Trouble, however, appeared on the horizon when the commissioner of police, Sir Richard Mayne, decided to arrest Napper and sent two of his plain-clothes men to Finchley for that purpose. Initially they hung around the bar at the Five Bells and brought up the subject of boxing but, being somewhat obvious, were not encouraged. They proceeded to question Ted when he came in from his morning walk, but he pretended to have no knowledge of this Napper who was fighting next week. Not being satisfied, the officers returned the following day and cunningly contrived to overhear a conversation which unfortunately implicated the pugilist, who was then speedily apprehended.

Napper's case was heard at Marylebone Police Court in front of a Mr Yardley on the Saturday before the encounter was due to take place. The magistrate proved to be very sympathetic to his cause and strongly condemned the underhand way in which he had been detained. To the amazement of Napper's friends in attendance, Mr Yardley announced that the boxer was "improperly in custody" and ordered him to be released immediately. Although all were gratified at this unexpected turn of events, the fact that there had been no binding over to keep the peace did highlight one particular problem. Convinced, after the arrest, that he would be prevented from meeting Hicken, Napper had indulged in a substantial meal of four or five eggs and a large rasher of bacon washed down with almost a quart of coffee. As a result, he found himself over the agreed weight limit and had to resort to heavy dosing with a purgative in order to remove the excess pounds. Surprisingly it did not seem to weaken him, nor did the pre-fight events affect his concentration, for his performance in the contest itself was conceivably the finest of his career. He emerged victorious after another protracted battle lasting 2 hours and 40 minutes, during which 88 severe rounds were eagerly contested.

Following a further win, against Jem Dove, in September 1864, Napper was inactive for over two years until a match was at length arranged with the heavier Jack Baldock of Islington. Since it was made at 9 stone 10 pounds, Ted was able, on this occasion, to eat well during his training although he still toiled hard under his martinet overseer, Nap Lawley. They began work at Woodford but, when the authorities became aware of the situation, were forced to move to Hammersmith and eventually once more to the Five Bells at Finchley. The bout, which proved to be both extremely unsportsmanlike and highly controversial, came off on 23 October 1866 at Hole Haven in Essex. It was marked by some of the most disgraceful episodes of foul play to be witnessed in the ring for many a long year. The combatants, when down, more than once refused to discontinue fighting, and incidents of kicking, gouging, biting and spiking were rife throughout. The behaviour of the seconds and supporters was, if anything, even worse and after 56 minutes the referee, fearing a general mêlée, wisely retired from the scene. The stakes were later given to Baldock, but the whole affair was singularly unsatisfactory and neither party emerged with any credit.

After an engagement with Sam Haley in January 1868 failed to take place owing to police interference, Napper, prior to retiring, made an unsuccessful offer to meet any man in the world at 9 stone 4 or 9 stone 6 pounds, for £200 to £500 a side. In April 1873 he tried his hand at glove combat (endurance) but was beaten by the holder, Michael (Charley) Davis, when challenging for the 11st Champion Cup. (This was one of three silver trophies donated by Messrs Lewis, Parnall, Preston and Richardson and first fought for at Bow a year earlier.) Napper continued to play an active part in the sport as trainer, second and backer until his much lamented death on 23 October 1879 at his public house, the Five Inkhorns in Shoreditch.

Tom Paddock Remains at Finchley

Finchley became the final resting place for the 'Redditch Needle-pointer', Tom Paddock, who mixed with virtually every big man of repute during the fifth decade of the 19th century. His professional career began in January 1844, when *Bell's Life in London* reported a purse fight at Mappleborough Green, after 'Tom the Greek' and Sam Simmonds had contended, which was "won by a Redditch man of hardy and game pretensions". Next came a victory over the much older Elijah

146

27. *Tom Paddock,*
the 'Redditch Needle-pointer'.

Parsons and two defeats of the skilful Nobby Clarke. Paddock was then thought capable enough to be pitted against 'Bendigo', who had regained the championship from Ben Caunt in a controversial bout in September 1845. The match took place at Mildenhall on 5 June 1850 and Tom, after being in a winning position, threw away his advantage, and eventually the contest, by his impetuosity. He was no more successful when facing William Perry ('Bendigo' having retired) in his second foray into the championship arena at the end of the same year. Once again Paddock's temper got the better of him and he was guilty of perpetrating a palpable foul in the 27th round.

Three desperate battles against Nottingham's Harry Poulson followed with Paddock avenging an initial loss by scoring two hard-earned successes. The riot which ensued during their second encounter resulted in the fighters being sentenced to ten months' imprisonment with hard labour, although neither man was involved in the disturbance. As far as Paddock was concerned, his forced confinement in Derby Gaol was not entirely to his disadvantage since it seemed to have had a beneficial effect on his headstrong disposition.

Another arduous struggle on 18 July 1854 saw Paddock overcome a determined Aaron Jones in 2 hours 24 minutes. The following month he intimated to *Bell's Life* that he thought it time that his claims to the championship were again put forward. Tom proceeded to throw down the gauntlet to both Perry and Harry Broome, being unsure which of them considered himself the champion, as the latter had previously beaten the 'Tipton Slasher' and then subsequently forfeited to him. The challenge was soon taken up by Broome, but the proposed meeting twice ended with him also forfeiting to Paddock. At this time *Bell's Life* informed its readers that, with regard to the title of champion of England, "Paddock can claim the distinction until it is wrested from him by the Tipton Slasher, Aaron Jones, or some other aspirant".

Jones fared no better in their rematch in June 1855 and, when a new championship belt was planned shortly afterwards, Broome decided to return to the ring to prove his entitlement to it. Articles were signed for him and Paddock to meet on 19 May 1856 and the winner, *Bell's Life* announced, would have "the honour of contending with the Tipton Slasher for the right of wearing the New Champion's Belt". The battle proved somewhat easier for Tom than had been generally anticipated since it quickly became apparent that his opponent had lost most of his former fighting abilities. Nevertheless it took 51 rounds before, utterly exhausted, Broome acknowledged that he had been beaten by a better man.

The year ended in bitter disappointment for Paddock when he was forced to forfeit to Perry because of want of backers and his own gambling excesses. The fortunate 'Slasher' was therefore considered indisputably the champion without the need to throw a single punch. However, when Tom Sayers surprisingly ended the seasoned veteran's reign, Paddock saw an opportunity to regain his laurels. His chance to do so was initially thwarted by serious illness but eventually went ahead on 15 June 1858. From the very beginning of the bout it was obvious that he had not fully recovered his physical powers, although his 'bottom' remained undiminished. An injury to Paddock's right hand must certainly have hindered him yet it was not a major factor in his honourable, but complete defeat.

Two years later, when the championship was in abeyance after the Sayers–Heenan contest, the massive Sam Hurst, a well-known Lancashire wrestler nicknamed the 'Stalybridge Infant', pressed his claim. This stirred Paddock to decide on a final attempt at fistic glory and a match was made between them, to take place on 6 November 1860 (not 5 November as sometimes erroneously stated), for £200 a side and the champion's belt. In the fifth round, a chance blow by Hurst broke two of Tom's ribs and so ended "an active, chequered but not inglorious Ring career".

Paddock did not live long to enjoy his well-earned retirement, dying from heart disease on 30 June 1863. On 5 July his remains were consigned to their final resting place at St Marylebone Cemetery, Finchley, and most of the London Ring were there to pay their last respects. As he departed in extremely impecunious circumstances, the Pugilistic Benevolent Association donated £5 towards the cost of the funeral. By a strange coincidence Paddock's wife, Esther Ann, was laid to rest in the same public grave; this unusual occurrence came about because she died shortly after her husband and was interred only nine days later.

Following the fighter's demise Alec Keene, a famous ex-lightweight and then a successful race-course caterer, raised a sum of money for Tom's widow which, after her untimely death, more than offset the cost of her funeral. It was suggested that the balance be used towards erecting a monument to the memory of Paddock, but it seems as though not enough donations were collected to make this a reality.

Jem Mace at the Five Bells

Few men have successfully reversed a poor early reputation more dramatically than the pugilist often considered the father of the modern scientific school of boxing, Jem Mace. An inexplicable 'bolting' before a proposed bout with Mike Madden and a dubious knockout defeat by Bob Brettle led *Bell's Life in London* to comment in January 1859 that he was "one of the most chicken hearted men that ever pulled a shirt off". Yet Mace went on to earn worldwide acclaim during a lengthy globe-trotting career. Indeed, the evergreen pugilist continued to hold his own in sparring sessions with respected performers less than half his age when well into his seventies.

Mace's connection with Finchley occurred in August 1863 when, under the supervision of Alf Milner of Sheffield and veteran Bob Bunn of Norwich, he repaired to the Five Bells before the first of his three encounters with Joe Goss. He had not fought since losing the English championship belt to Tom King in November of the previous year and this contest was therefore a significant one as he sought to re-establish his lost standing. (Although Jem still regarded himself as the champion, King having briefly retired after their bout, *Bell's Life* stated that the belt was to remain in their possession "until Mace shall

28. *Jem Mace,*
generally regarded as the father of the
modern scientific school of boxing.

either have again earned it in battle array, or until some other aspirant shall have made good his claim to it". However, the Goss match-up could not be for the championship since the participants were confined to a weight limit, namely 10 stone 10 pounds.)

Mace worked extremely hard at Finchley and the *Sporting Life* reported that he covered some forty miles a day "in pedestrian exercise". As a result *Bell's Life* of 23 August was of the opinion that he was "bang up to the mark and under his weight", whilst the *Sporting Life* of the previous day believed Mace to be half a pound below his target. According to Mace's memoirs this was, in fact, completely incorrect. The easy life he had led since the King fight had resulted in his becoming rather fleshy and, despite the strenuous exertions undertaken, two days before the weigh-in he was still almost four pounds too heavy. Mace told of the extreme measures to which he was subjected in order to avoid forfeiting the substantial stake money. For 48 hours he was allowed neither food nor drink, whilst all the time being confined to a room where two large fires were kept going all day and night. In addition, he was covered in blankets which "formed a heap that reached nearly to the ceiling". He felt his suffering to have been worthwhile, for he succeeded in turning the scale at one and a quarter ounces under the stipulated limit.

Whilst at the Five Bells, Mace was joined by Jack Lead, the elder and better known of two boxing brothers, who was scheduled to meet Young George Holden of Walsall following the big fight. He was backed from Jem's public house in Holywell Lane, Shoreditch, and Mace assisted in his training along with Bunn and another Norwich man by the name of Loakes. Lead was confined to 8 stone, which he made without difficulty, and his overall condition reflected well on all concerned.

On 1 September a ring was set up at Wootton Bassett, but hardly had the great £1000 battle between Mace and Goss begun than the police put in an unwelcome appearance. Eventually the fight was resumed at Long Reach, and after a total of 19 often cautious rounds, lasting 1 hour 55 ½ minutes, Mace delivered a tremendous right-hand blow which knocked his opponent completely insensible. The Lead–Holden contest had to be postponed until the next day when it was also interrupted by police as the combatants were scratching for the 45th round. At that point, with the Walsall man too punished to renew hostilities, Lead was declared a worthy winner.

Mace himself may have visited Finchley again in the early years of the present century, but this time under much sadder circumstances. On 27 January 1908 his much younger wife, Alice Caroline, died in Islington and was buried two days later in nonconformist ground in the borough's cemetery at Finchley. Although the *Sporting Life* claimed in Mace's obituary that his spouse's death distressed him greatly, it seems strange that the wording on her tombstone reads "Dear Mother" only. Moreover the *Mirror of Life* mentioned that she left four young children in an impoverished situation, and so it is quite possible that she was estranged from her husband.

The 'Royal Professor'

"He who can, does. He who cannot teaches". When the venerable dramatist George Bernard Shaw wrote these words, he obviously did not have in mind his old boxing tutor, Ned Donnelly. Shaw retained an enormous respect for the ex-prize-ring practitioner whose gym in Panton Street, Haymarket, he had frequented as a penniless young man. In fact, the character of the trainer in *Cashel Byron's Profession* (Shaw's novel on the noble art which contained uncanny similarities to world heavyweight champion Gene Tunney's career some half a century later) owed much, as the writer himself acknowledged, to the man considered the premier pugilistic 'professor' of his age.

Unlike his namesake from Glasgow, this particular Ned Donnelly did not compile an extensive fight record in the bareknuckle arena. Hailing from Somers Town (a district near London's King's Cross), he first came to notice when, on 12 January 1864, he outclassed Paddington's Jem Styles in a minor mill of ten rounds lasting a mere 16 minutes. The *Illustrated Sporting News* of 16 January related that, prior to the bout, Donnelly had "trained at Barnet where Warwick, the King-Maker, was killed in Edward's time". Unfortunately the newspaper did not print any further details, although this is understandable since its subject was yet to make his reputation in the field in which he would later become a household name. Donnelly himself subsequently confirmed that he was "trained carefully at Barnet" before defeating Styles, but again did not elaborate.

A match 18 months later with Tom M'Kelvey appears to have been Donnelly's last without the gloves. Only three years afterwards he was instructing at Nat Langham's Mitre public house in St Martin's Lane, London, where he was billed as the "most noted teacher of his day". He is known to have stayed at Whetstone in June 1868, when training Tom Goller for a contest with Nat Bowler on the 29th of that month. (Goller was "perfectly fit for his task" and was declared the winner after contending for exactly one hour.)

Donnelly's manual on self-defence, which first appeared in 1879, went through at least five editions and was regarded by enthusiasts of the fistic art to be the best-ever of its kind. However, Donnelly did not pen the work himself for he could neither read nor write. This gave rise to an amusing incident when, at the very time ownership of his book was deemed essential for any serious exponent of the sport, its renowned author was espied poring over an upside-down copy of *The Referee* newspaper. According to Louis Cohen, a well-known diamond speculator and writer, Donnelly was a "funny h-less cove, with his round rubicund face, raw chin, bright eyes, top hat, innocent ignorance and worldly wisdom". (Cohen knew the former pugilist well since Donnelly, at one period, frequently took him and the mining magnate Barney Barnato on Sunday jaunts to the Welsh Harp.)

Known as the 'Royal Professor' on account of his having performed in front of royalty several times, Donnelly taught, as stated in an advertisement for his Haymarket establishment, 24 winners of the Marquess of Queensberry's Cups. He even had an indirect hand in producing the first scientific heavyweight of the modern age, since one of his assistants later became the instructor at the Olympic Club in San Francisco when James J Corbett was initially learning his craft. However, somewhat surprisingly, in view of his immense popularity and the number of affluent students of whom he could boast, Donnelly's life in retirement was far from comfortable. He was forced to exist on a small annuity presented to him by H J Chinnery, an outstanding amateur and former pupil. Although his name is largely unknown to today's boxing

29. The 'Royal Professor', Ned Donnelly, the most distinguished pugilistic teacher of his age.

fans, Donnelly's contribution during the early period of the gloved era was highly significant. Indeed the comment by B J Angle that he was a "man to whom British boxing owes far more than history will ever be able to tell" is not too far wide of the mark.

Hell Hath No Fury ...

Despite the meticulous attentions of those appointed to look after them, many a hot-blooded fighter fell victim to the comely charms of a local lass whilst preparing for a forthcoming fistic engagement. Although the bruiser involved invariably considered the liaison to be little more than a welcome diversion from the rigours of training, the lady in question sometimes viewed matters more seriously. Such a situation appears to have arisen in March 1865 when Tim Collins, who in the three years since his ring introduction had shown himself to be a competent young performer, set up camp at Lewes in Sussex prior to his match with Bob Furze. Certainly the boxer was forced to leave his quarters in a considerable hurry a fortnight earlier than had originally been intended owing to police interference. *Gale's Licensed Victuallers' Mirror*, in its series 'Chronicles of the Prize Ring', believed that the hasty flight had been "caused through information supplied by one of Collins's 'friends'; a young lady who doubtless thought herself badly used by him and perhaps had been".

Along with his trainer, Nat Langham's stud groom, Collins found alternative accommodation at Finchley's popular Five Bells public house. There the finishing touches were put to his conditioning. He obviously applied himself assiduously to these latter stages of preparation as at the weigh-in he managed to scale inside the 8 stone 4 pound limit. This was no mean feat since, for his weight, Collins was a somewhat tall man with excellent muscular development. However, despite his belated dedication, on 15 April he suffered the second and final setback of his career, Furze being declared the winner after 49 rounds. Their initial meeting two days earlier had been interrupted by police.

The loser scored several subsequent victories, including twice beating Brighton's Bill Gillam on a profitable day at Reading Races. He then took the decision to join the pugilistic exodus to the United States where lucrative opportunities awaited those who displayed a modicum of milling ability. Shortly after his arrival he was said to have been responsible for causing the brawl in a New York tavern which resulted in the fatal stabbing of Felix Larkin, the American backer of the giant Irishman Ned (O') Baldwin. Collins later put his belligerent tendencies to better use when, in May 1871, he drew with Billy Edwards for the lightweight championship of America. Along with the majority of the pugilists who left England at the time, he never returned. On 30 October 1886 the *Chicago Tribune* mentioned that he lay dying in the Northampton (Mass) Lunatic Asylum after alcohol had made him a "physical and mental wreck".

A Romany Encounter

"In times gone by the vicinity of a fair or racecourse was chosen to settle the differences between the professors of the art pugilistique – the last Barnet Fair revived the custom". So commented the *Illustrated Sporting and Theatrical News* of 14 September 1867 before detailing a grudge battle between a couple of fighting Romanies named Mark Howard and Ben Cooper. These men had fought twice before, originally contending for 'love' (a somewhat inappropriate term since there was obviously little affection between them) and, on the second occasion, for a sovereign a side. This third encounter was arranged for £10 and took place "after Barnet Races", somewhere in the general vicinity of the town. The *Illustrated Sporting and Theatrical News* and *Bell's Life in London* disagreed about the precise day. The former recorded the contest as occurring on Monday 9 September and the latter two days earlier. At least 500 people were present for the match, which reminded the old-timers of bygone days for the onlookers came "on horses, ponies, donkeys, and in every kind of traps [*sic*]".

The protagonists' previous clashes had been casual turn-ups and this affair, planned two weeks before, gave them a chance for the first time to fit in some brief training before meeting one another. On stripping, Howard, the taller man by two inches at 5 feet 4, looked in the better condition. He was also equipped with fighting boots while his opponent wore only thin shoes. However, despite his inferior appearance and the disadvantage of such unsuitable footwear on an extremely slippery ground, Cooper was the initial betting favourite. Bob Webb, whose boxing booth was a regular feature at Barnet Fair, was appointed as referee and, with a certain Billy Pea keeping order at ringside, the Romany encounter commenced.

The moment the combatants appeared at the scratch it was evident that they were far from novices, and the science displayed was considerably more than expected. In the third round the favourite gained first blood and for 30 minutes managed to sustain a definite lead. Unusually, since he was the weaker man, Cooper particularly excelled in wrestling but this ultimately proved to be his downfall; in executing a cross-buttock throw he so severely injured his right arm that it was entirely useless for the remainder of the bout. The odds immediately veered around and Howard soon after assumed control. He scored the first knock-down in the seventh round and from then onwards proceeded to dominate against his game but struggling opponent. Cooper, obviously fighting to order (the well-known Jack Hicks and Mike Cocklin were attending him), repeatedly dropped without a blow being struck and was frequently cautioned for this offence. Eventually, following 2 hours 4 minutes of action, for the last 90 minutes of which Cooper had been reduced to performing one-handed, referee Webb awarded victory to Howard after his opponent had yet again gone down suspiciously.

During the 42-round contest the winner was much punished about the body, whilst Cooper suffered a considerable amount of head damage. Despite the loser's tendency to drop illegally, *Bell's Life* was moved to comment that "a gamer man never stripped".

Resting-place for Lightweight Heroes

Frank Redmond was another pugilist buried at Finchley of whom mention should be made, for he was well respected first as a determined lightweight and later as a successful publican. Indeed he could be considered a true member of the Fancy – this term was not always restricted to those who followed or were involved in the prize-ring but was, on occasions, extended to include "sporting in general", and here Redmond's knowledge could scarcely be equalled.

Redmond's fight record perhaps did not entirely do him justice. Of the four battles in which he participated, he emerged triumphant in just one, his last, against Tom Davis on 14 November 1833. However, in his two setbacks against the famed Barney Aaron he exhibited tremendous gameness and in their second meeting, in October 1827, the speed and force of his hits gave him an excellent chance of victory right up until the latter stages of the 42-round contest.

Eventually though, as had been the case in their more one-sided bout four years before, the superior strength and ability of the 'Star of the East' proved decisive. Redmond's other defeat, as has been previously mentioned, came at the hands of the 'Sailor Boy', Harry Jones, following a manly encounter of 36 minutes at No Mans Land on 31 March 1829.

Shortly after his solitary win, Redmond became landlord of the George and Dragon in Greek Street, situated at the heart of London's Soho district. He soon attracted a considerable sports-orientated clientele for, as well as a growing reputation as a first-rate teacher of the noble art, he had also acquired a detailed understanding of the finer points of the canine species. Redmond later moved to the Swiss Cottage in St John's Wood, where he continued to command loyal support from his previous customers. He was by then acknowledged as one of the country's leading dog-fanciers, a fact noted in an extremely favourable write-up his establishment received in an 1846 publication, *Walks around London*. This also offered the opinion that the "Swiss Cottage at the intersection of the London and Finchley Roads and Belsize Lane, is a pleasant summer retreat; and it would be hard to name a more competent authority on sporting subjects than the worthy host".

30. *The grave of a true member of the Fancy, Frank Redmond. (Reproduced by kind permission of Westminster City Council.)*

Redmond died, aged 69, at 15 Abbey Road West, St John's Wood, on 23 February 1871. He was interred six days later at St Marylebone Cemetery, Finchley, in a family tomb containing several of his close relatives. (His inscription on the gravestone, right, is the one third from bottom.)

The other lightweight hero to be buried at Finchley during the 1870s was Jem Gollagher, born of Irish parents in the neighbourhood of Somers Town in 1842. After a few rough turn-ups as a youth, he made a successful ring début by defeating a 13-stone novice whose name has been unrecorded for posterity. His next encounter was a desperate one with (Professor) Bill Jones on 9 March 1861, in which Gollagher prevailed in 100 rounds, lasting precisely two hours. This led to his match exactly four months later with Aaron Moss, who claimed to be distantly related to the celebrated 'Young Dutch Sam' and boxed under the same appellation. In his most important battle to date, Jem proved himself to be a lad of considerable promise, impressing those watching by determinedly overcoming his opponent's strong early lead and eventually gaining the upper hand. At the end of 64 rounds he was so completely in control of the bout that Moss's seconds, seeing the hopeless nature of the struggle, humanely retired their man.

On 27 November 1862, Gollagher drew with the renowned Jack Hicks after a 58-round fight twice suspended by police interference. His continued improvement was much in evidence when, in July the following year, he easily beat Jem Dove in a mere ten minutes. Thereafter, however, his career suffered a serious setback. A broken piece of china, thrown by a child, severely damaged his right eye and he was not seen in the ring again until meeting Abe Hicken on 24 May 1866. In the ninth round, as both men sparred for an opening, a charge was made by four policemen who advanced upon the boxers. The referee immediately ordered Gollagher and Hicken to take flight, a command with which they were happy to comply. In what proved to be Jem's last contest, they later agreed to draw the stakes.

As proprietor of a sporting house, the Jolly Friar off Blackfriars Road, Gollagher continued to maintain strong links with the prize-ring. There he organized what was somewhat exaggeratedly advertised as the "finest sparring in London, conducted by the Light-weight Champion himself, the scientific Jem Gollagher". In the grand tradition of the best pugilistic publicans, he was always ready to help the less fortunate and, in December 1867, set up a subscription for the orphaned children of the recently deceased Jack Grant.

Gollagher passed away at his residence in Burton Street, St Pancras, on 13 October 1874. A post-mortem carried out upon the wishes of his brother, found the cause of death to have been "rheumatism of the heart". Previous to his untimely demise he had been employed by Alec Keene and his partner, George Brown, in their thriving catering business. Gollagher was buried on 19 October, under his real name of James Gallagher, in a public grave in St Pancras Cemetery. (This was the first of Finchley's three major burial grounds, established after the 1852 Metropolitan Interment Act gave London vestries the power to create boards to set up new cemeteries of their own. It was built on land previously belonging to Horseshoe Farm on Finchley Common and shortly afterwards a portion was sold off to form Islington Cemetery.) The funeral was attended by a great number of Jem's friends and associates and the procession covered nearly a

31. The first-class unbeaten lightweight, Jem Gollagher.

quarter of a mile. The boxing fraternity was well represented by many lighter-weight fighters who were contemporaries of the deceased, including Tommy Hackett, Harry Rackham, Tom Goller, Tommy Hogan, George Flynn, George Gregg and Gollagher's old opponent, Professor Jones. As a mark of respect, every shop in Somers Town closed for the afternoon.

Webb's Boxing Booth

The presence of a booth exhibiting the manly art at traditional English fairs dates back to the old days of James Figg. A reproduction of a handbill advertising "FIG'S [*sic*] GREAT TIL'D BOOTH, On the Bowling-Green, Southwark, During the Time of the Fair" can be found in the first volume of *Boxania*. This announced that 'Buckhorse' (a noted character more famous for his hardiness than ability) and several other bruisers would "shew the Art of Boxing" and Figg himself would "exhibit his knowledge in various Combats – with the Foil, Back-sword, Cudgel, and Fist". Indeed Hogarth featured Figg in the foreground of his celebrated work 'Southwark Fair': he is depicted mounted on a miserable nag and his bald head is covered with black patches, indicating the scars left from his many confrontations. Nearly a century and a half later, as the bareknuckle era drew to a close, the fair-ground boxing booth continued to be a popular draw. However, the premier outfit was no longer run by a prominent figure but by Bob Webb who, during his fighting career, was little more than a good trial horse.

Webb's only two recorded contests were a desperate losing battle against the top class Job Cobley in March 1856 and a victory over Dan Liddell in July the following year. He was by all accounts a stylish pugilist, a point endorsed by the *Illustrated Sporting News* of 24 January 1863, which reported that Nat Langham was sparring in Dublin with the "very artistic boxer Bob Webb". In August 1858 he was advertised as being the director of boxing at the White Horse, Baldwin's Gardens, Holborn, and in the new year of 1866 he assumed control of that iniquitous establishment. It was, though, as the proprietor of a booth which visited virtually every fair in the country that Webb was probably best known.

It is certain that, for several years at least, Webb's itinerary included Barnet Fair. In September 1870 the *Barnet Press* described a slight altercation between "an individual endeavouring to induce people to buy penny purses for a shilling and the principal of Bob Webb's boxing booth". Wisely the ex-pugilist's adversary was content to keep the hostilities on a purely verbal footing. The unsavoury language expressed, however, was apparently impressive, even by the time-honoured standards of the fair-ground.

32. A boxing booth at Barnet Fair at a later date than Bob Webb's sparring saloon but still featuring a bareknuckle backdrop. (Reproduced by kind permission of Barnet Museum.)

A further mention of Webb at Barnet Fair can be found in the same newspaper four years later, whilst a sparring saloon referred to in its 1875 and 1876 reports of the event was most probably his also. In 1876 the unnamed owner of the booth was charging a two pence admission fee to witness a display that he audaciously described as being between "two of the greatest prize-fighters in the world".

Ill-health was responsible for ending Webb's travelling days. According to *Bell's Life* he died on 17 April 1878, the bitter weather of the previous month having brought on the attack of bronchitis to which he eventually succumbed.

From Knuckles to Gloves

In their 1901 book *The National Sporting Club Past and Present*, A F Bettinson and W Tristram Outram related how the former had been one of the backers involved in a prize-ring bout at Hadley Wood. No date was mentioned but it is clear from the *Sporting Life* (despite some discrepancies between the two sources) that the contest must have taken place on 18 August 1881. The encounter was for £25 a side and the combatants two inexperienced but competent young fighters, namely Harry Crook of Camden Town and James Gleeson of Somers Town.

The 21-year-old Gleeson, who had shown his mettle in a determined mill with Thomas Galvin of Ballincolla the previous April, stood 5 feet 5 inches tall and weighed, on the day, 8 stone 2 pounds. He was in peak condition, having trained at Brighton under the watchful eye of 'Punch' Callow who, the year before, had drawn with the renowned Birmingham lightweight Jem Carney. Gleeson's opponent, Crook, was only one year older and half an inch taller, but had the advantage of ten pounds in weight. His preparation had also gone well and, for those in the know, a "rare treat" was anticipated.

On reaching the intended destination, a 16-foot ring was pitched in a "delightful spot" which had been carefully selected because it was well screened by trees from unwanted observation. No time was lost in getting the battle under way, and the action from the start was fierce and committed. Gleeson drew first blood in round three and seemed to be establishing a lead when the appearance of several policemen brought matters to a temporary halt. The *Sporting Life* reported that this interference came about after nine brief rounds, whereas Bettinson and Outram remembered the interruption as occurring at the end of just four. Both, though, emphasized that the arrival of the unwelcome visitors resulted in the usual general panic.

All interested parties reassembled at Potters Bar, but the forces of law and order intervened again before resumption of hostilities could take place. The thwarted gathering next decided upon a short railway journey to Oakleigh Park. However, the proposed plan to resurrect proceedings there had to be hastily abandoned when it was discovered that the train they had boarded was not scheduled to stop at that station. Undeterred, they alighted at Wood Green where the advice of a local fistic sage was eagerly sought. Harry Brunton, the former faithful second of Tom Sayers, listened sympathetically to their catalogue of disasters and then suggested a nearby spot where the affair could be renewed without further disturbance.

In a secluded part of Alexandra Park the protagonists once more enthusiastically set to. By the 17th round Crook looked to be thoroughly beaten and Jack Hicks, in Gleeson's corner, instructed his man to go in and gain the victory. Crook, though, recovered remarkably well and eventually began to force the fighting. In the 43rd round he delivered a right-hand blow which appeared to render his opponent completely unconscious. Somehow Gleeson managed to stagger to the scratch when 'time' was next called and bravely hurled himself back into the fray. In fact so determinedly did he rally that he succeeded in knocking Crook down in each of the following four rounds. At this point Crook's second, the well-known Islington pugilist Peter Brislin, conceded the contest and Gleeson was proclaimed a worthy winner. From the customary early-morning start it had taken the entire day to bring matters to a satisfactory conclusion and Bettinson wrote that it was not until seven o'clock in the evening that he was able to put the vanquished hero into a hot bath.

Not satisfied with the defeat, Crook hankered after a chance for revenge and was duly delighted when the opportunity was presented to him the following year. A purse was collected for which the pair could contend, but on this occasion the match was fought with small gloves under the Marquess of Queensberry's rules for endurance. It took place on 22 February 1882 and was distinguished by the courage, determination and fairness shown by both sides. At length, after 2 hours 15 minutes, a draw was suggested and, the men being willing, they shook hands and divided the purse. Crook lived until as late as 1933, and was buried in Islington Cemetery, Finchley.

Undercover Operation

For some time prior to Wednesday 5 December 1883, talk was rife in sporting circles that a prize-fight was being arranged in the London area and that two capable boxers had gone into strict training for the contest. The rumours were confirmed on the Tuesday evening when a meeting was held between the friends of each man. The decision was then taken that the bout, which was to be for £20 a side, would commence at seven o'clock the next morning at Hadley Wood.

The following day Edward Ryan and William Williams were amongst the passengers leaving King's Cross on two early-morning trains out of the metropolis. Williams, a 29-year-old horse-keeper, and Ryan, a tailor four years his junior, were, according to both *Bell's Life* and *The Times*, "well known in London as pugilists", although their previous achievements appear to be undocumented. Alighting at New Barnet Station, the fighters and their supporters proceeded, by what was known as the 'railway path', to Hadley Wood. No ropes or stakes being available, the spectators stood shoulder to shoulder to form a ring and, soon after the appointed time, the men prepared for action. It was clear that both had benefited from rigorous conditioning but Williams looked in every way the superior and this was strongly reflected in the betting.

Ryan commenced in a very cautious vein and was careful to avoid coming to close quarters. Matters livened up considerably, though, when Williams succeeded in landing heavily on his opponent's nose and a spirited rally ensued in which the tailor found himself at a decided disadvantage. This lasted, so the *Dundee Courier and Argus* of the next day reported, nearly two minutes. (It was not that unusual for the Scottish press to keep their readers abreast of major English prize-ring activities but, strangely for such an obscure fight, the newspaper printed more actual details than its London counterparts.) With Ryan being knocked all over the ring, his backers began to become extremely anxious but even they could not have been pleased at the abrupt turn of events that saved their man from almost certain defeat.

On 'time' being called for the second round, the hostilities were suddenly rudely interrupted by an invasion of constables who had been lying in wait close by. Unbeknown to the fight contingent a certain Inspector Cole, in charge of Barnet police, had earlier received information from London of the impending encounter and had organized a body of his men to be hidden in the wood. At a given signal they sprang from their hiding places and, in the regular stampede that followed, managed to capture both participants and several spectators. The detainees, 11 in number, were speedily conveyed to Barnet police station and shortly afterwards brought up at the magistrates' clerk's office before one Major Adair. The charge against Williams and Ryan was that of committing a breach of the peace by taking part in a prize-fight, and against the others of aiding and abetting such a contest.

Once the formal evidence had been presented, the prisoners were given the opportunity to speak up for themselves and showed great imagination in justifying their situation. Ryan maintained that he and Williams had argued in the street and agreed to settle their differences in the time-honoured tradition of fistic combat. He was adamant that they had not been engaged in a prize-fight and alleged the spectators were merely friends who had come to see fair play. Richard Wilson, a painter from Turnham Green, stated that he and a barman named Nick Thompson had heard in a London public house that a three-round glove contest was being arranged and decided to go along to see it. Laughter erupted when he stressed that, had they known it was going to be an illegal bareknuckle affair, they would of course have kept away. William Ryan, a 28-year-old tobacconist, said he had been arrested whilst innocently walking towards the wood and insisted that he had not been present at the fight, even though his brother was involved. Their inventiveness, however, failed to impress and all were remanded in custody until the following Monday. Bail was refused on the grounds that every one of them was a stranger to the neighbourhood and, in the course of the afternoon, they were removed to Holloway Prison.

On 10 December the 11 prisoners were brought up before a full bench of magistrates at High Barnet police court. Considerable interest was shown in the proceedings and the building was extremely crowded. The prisoners were duly committed for trial at the next sessions of the Central Criminal Court and bail was set at £100 each for the principals and £40 each for the others. At the conclusion, the bench recorded its admiration at the clever manner by which the capture had been effected and praised Inspector Cole for his efficient organisation.

The men surrendered to take their trial on 11 January the following year. Mr Horace Avory, the counsel for the prosecution, opened the case by explaining that the offence with which the prisoners were charged was that of being involved in a prize-fight. However, as a fight of any kind was considered a breach of the peace, there were only two questions upon which the jury needed to reflect. These were whether the affair had actually happened and whether all the defendants were guilty of being present, either as participants or active supporters. He proceeded to describe the events leading up to the successful apprehension of the prisoners and stated that there could be no doubt that an affray had taken place. Both Williams and Ryan were bleeding when arrested and the police had seized possession of two sponges used to tend the protagonists, one of which was marked with blood. It was also apparent to him that the other nine men detained had journeyed specifically to Barnet and knew exactly what was to occur. Several police constables were called and gave testimonies supporting Mr Avory's contentions.

At the end of the prosecution's case, the counsels for the combatants, aware that evidence against their clients was overwhelming, decided to plead guilty. However, Mr Keith Frith on behalf of Charles Thomas, a bootmaker from Grosvenor Square, argued there was no proof that his client had in any way instigated or encouraged the encounter. Thomas's explanation was that, attracted by the noise, he had been in attendance as an accidental onlooker only and in no other capacity than out of mere curiosity. William Ryan then caused great amusement by pointing out that, even if the jury thought him to have been present, there was no reason for them to believe he had not intended to obstruct rather than assist with the fight.

After Mr Justice Hawkins had summed up, the jury retired to consider their decision; a few minutes later they returned, having found a verdict of guilty against all the accused. In passing sentence, the judge took a lenient view since the prisoners had not resisted or obstructed the police in the execution of their duty. They were all ordered to pay £5, to enter into their own recognizances in the sum of £50, and to find one surety of £25 to keep the peace and be of good behaviour for a year. Four of the defendants being unable to pay the fine, the judge, not wishing to send them to prison, allowed the men one calendar month to settle. Whilst some sections of the press praised him for his sensible handling of the case, others voiced their concern over his apparent sympathy towards the accused who, they felt, could congratulate themselves on the lightness of their sentences.

A minor footnote to the affair came in May 1933 when a Mr Alfred S Mays gave a lecture to the then Barnet Record Society entitled 'Some Notes on the Barnet Police Force'. Basing his talk on a diary that his father had kept, he told how Police Constable Charles Mays had attended the Old Bailey to give evidence against the 11 men involved. Interestingly, there was also a further reference in the diary to "duty in Hadley Wood looking for prize fighters".

Fair Trickery

An entertaining character known to frequent Barnet Fair during the latter part of the 19th century was George Dove, who in his younger days had been a talented bantamweight in both the prize-ring and early gloved competitions. As a teenager, Dove was a popular performer in most of the East End of London's sparring saloons, particularly Bill Richardson's famous Blue Anchor at Shoreditch. At length he was matched against Bill Lead, the brother of the more renowned Jack, with whom he consented to a draw (despite having the upper hand) after their contest had been interrupted by police. His only other bareknuckle encounter was against Woolf Cohen, a promising young boxer being put forward at that time by the Jewish sporting fraternity as their new representative. This battle, which took place on 3 July 1866, resulted in an impressive victory for the smaller Dove after 2 hours and 8 1/2 minutes of extended milling. Dove later donned the gloves at the Prince of Wales Grounds, Bow, to win the newly donated 8st 4lb cup and was hailed by *Bell's Life in London* as "Feather-weight Champion of Great Britain".

On retiring, Dove looked for an alternative means of livelihood where his quick hands and natural dexterity could be put to good use. He eventually chose the decidedly precarious calling of 'sharper', and Barnet Fair became one of his favourite hunting grounds. There Dove could be spotted, perched on a stool, performing coin tricks with considerable adroitness, whilst at the same time keeping up an amusing and extremely effective patter. He was, in the opinion of one who had witnessed his act many times, "a perfect master at the business", and as a result he no doubt made a reasonable living from his endeavours. Of course there was always the occupational hazard of the angry victim but then the ex-fighter was well equipped to cope with any violent repercussions that his artful ventures might have produced. Nevertheless, it is known that on one occasion at least he suffered a beating at the hands of a large countryman, who demonstrated his dissatisfaction in no uncertain manner.

It is probable that Dove could have become proficient at a more acceptable occupation had he shown the same amount of commitment that he displayed as a trickster. However, although there must have been easier ways of making a living, he appeared quite happy with his situation. One of the last surviving members of the old prize-ring, Dove expired, following a short illness, at the London Hospital in December 1895. Shortly after his demise the *Mirror of Life* paid tribute to the memory of "one of the gamest bantam weight boxers who ever put up his hands within a ringed enclosure".

Hatton's Hospitality Caravanserai

Hospitality booths run by former bareknuckle pugilists became a customary feature at Barnet Fair and Races during the second half of the 19th century (*see also* Appendix B). These served a mouthwatering array of joints, poultry and game and had on offer a wide variety of the best wines, spirits and ales available at the time. Amongst the most indefatigable of the ex-boxers to enter this field of catering was Jesse Hatton. Billing himself as the "famed Champion of Kent", he was a familiar sight at Barnet Fair for well over thirty years.

As a fighter, Hatton was not of the first rank but his gameness was unquestioned, his milling career being characterized by battles fought on the unscientific, albeit entertaining, give-and-take principle. In all, according to *Fistiana*, he participated in ten regular prize-ring bouts (losing six) during an eight-year stretch which ended in a defeat by the capable Mickey Gannon in April 1862. At that time Jesse was the landlord of the Champion Stores in Marylebone, but by 1864 he had moved to his "celebrated West End Resort" of the (Old) King's Head in Leicester Square. The date that he first began pitching his catering tent at Barnet Fair cannot be confirmed but it appears, if the memory of Hatton himself was correct, to have been prior to his retirement from boxing. (In September 1896 he told *Gale's Licensed Victuallers' Mirror* that he had "occupied the same ground at Barnet for thirty six years".)

In 1892, towards the end of his long association with the fair, disaster struck when a fire which had begun in an adjoining booth completely destroyed his tent and virtually all his stock. A willing crowd gathered to help but proceeded to relieve him of what was left of his property, whilst to add to the veteran's woes his waistcoat containing money and a watch and chain was also stolen. However, the boxing world rallied round and a benefit was duly arranged; sufficient funds were raised for a new booth, which Hatton used for the first time when visiting Epsom during Derby week of 1893.

Although by 1896 Jesse's health was failing, he was still determined to continue his catering duties whenever possible, and later that year was back at Barnet Fair once more. On 4 September *Gale's Licensed Victuallers' Mirror* informed its readers that Hatton had "secured a pitch – the old one – for his caravanserai, and if its ample dimensions cannot be made out by the near sighted, a sniff or two of sage and onion will lead to a spot where a wonderful pair of spectacles will be discovered resting somewhat aslant on a wonderful nose". Such a complimentary write-up must surely have boosted trade, but sadly this visit proved to be Hatton's last. He died in August 1897 and was buried in a public grave on the 12th of that month in Islington Cemetery, Finchley.

Boxing 'Bosses' at the Belgrave Tavern

The habitual progression from prize-fighter to licensed victualler has already been noted, but of the area's many 18th- and 19th-century drinking establishments only one had pugilistic 'managerial' links. This was the Belgrave Tavern, High Road, sometimes known as the High Street, (North) Finchley, which during its existence as a beer-house could boast two ex-boxers at its helm, William Springall and Bill Lee.

In his prime Springall was a powerful fighter with a devastating right hand and the appearance of a "barn door in boots". Indeed, his formidable strength and hitting power would doubtless have gained him considerable fame and fortune in the prize-ring, but by the time he came to the fore its popularity as a sport lay in the distant past. He is reputed to have fought once with the 'raw'uns', obtaining a 20-minute victory over one Jim Bolton at Battersea early in his career. This, though, cannot be substantiated, and as such must be considered rather questionable. What is certain, however, is that in October 1884 Springall was charged with aiding and abetting two of his former opponents, Jack Massey and William 'Coddy' Middings, in a prize-fight near Epsom. (He was found guilty, but the jury recommended leniency and he was released on his own recognizance.) Springall was a respected boxing 'professor'; one of his most famous pupils was Jem Kendrick, whose bareknuckle exploits included a somewhat unexpected 34-round victory over the determined battler Bill Cheese.

33. *William Springall, a notable middleweight and boxing 'professor'.*

(Reproduced by kind permission of Mrs Daisy Durrant.)

With the gloves Springall proved himself a first-class performer, winning Walter Watson and Bob Habbijam's 11st competition on 7 November 1882 by knocking out Massey in the final. This not inconsiderable achievement gained him recognition, at least by the *Sporting Life*, as "the 11st. champion". His fame was not merely confined to England, for in 1885 he impressed during a visit to the United States. Although unable to secure a match with any of the top middleweights, Springall nevertheless demonstrated sufficient ability to earn the *New York Herald's* praise as "not only a very scientific pugilist but a terrific hitter". On 23 February, backed and seconded by the former English and American bareknuckle lightweight champion Arthur Chambers, he had the better of a bout with the Brooklyn heavyweight Joe Denning before police intervened. He was later unfairly denied a decision in Philadelphia, but recorded an indisputable victory on 11 May, in his last overseas contest, against George Rooke, a distinguished Irish veteran of the American prize-ring.

Liverpool-born and originally billed as coming from Brighton, Springall appears in the 1881 census returns as a boiler-maker in London, living in Power Street, Battersea. In January 1883 he opened the short-lived South-Western School of Arms at the Victoria Hotel in the same area, and at the end of that year went to Peru to assist in the erecting of a new pier. It was the financial success of his American trip, however, which enabled Springall to become a licensed victualler. In October 1885 he began trading at the Queen, Wandsworth Road, Clapham, where he resuscitated his school of arms. Renowned for his generosity, he organized benefit evenings at his "well-conducted hostelry" for fellow members of the fistic fraternity such as Harry Hopkins and 'Deaf' Boome. (At the latter's, Springall sparred "three merry rounds" with 'Smoky' Bishop, who had been his pupil Kendrick's prize-ring début opponent.) He was still in the Wandsworth Road when the 1891 census was taken; the Kelly's directory for the Barnet area records him at the Belgrave Tavern for the first time in its 1894-5 publication.

Once ensconced in his new premises, Springall appears to have ceased arranging either boxing exhibitions or benefits. This was probably because the location would not have attracted the patronage of his former South London supporters. He did not enjoy good health at the Tavern and was ill for some time before dying there on 10 July 1898. He was only 46 years of age; the cause of his demise was given on his death certificate as bronchitis and diabetes. Springall was laid to rest four days later, the burial ground being, as the *Mirror of Life* related, Finchley's "well-kept Saint Marylebone Cemetery". An entry in the 1898-9 Kelly's directory indicates that his widow continued in business at the Belgrave Tavern after his death. Certainly the Mrs Bessie Saunders that the late C O Banks, a local historian, mentioned as its occupier at the turn of the century was the same lady, by then remarried.

William King, the Belgrave Tavern's other boxing 'boss', was known in pugilistic circles as Bill Lee, and had shown initial promise as a potential champion. However, he did not fully live up to expectations before the handicap of easily damaged hands precipitated his early ring retirement. The *Mirror of Life*, in a brief synopsis of his career after its premature conclusion, stated that he had participated in two bareknuckle affairs (wins over Alf Smith and Jack Barlow), but again these cannot be traced. Moreover, they are not mentioned in *Fighting Days*, in which Lee himself related incidents in his life to the book's author, Philip Drackett. In common with Springall, though, Lee did have a connection with Jack Massey, who had arranged his successful endurance match with 'Darkey' Burwick in November 1890 and seconded him in a loss against Ted Dutton in April of the following year. Lee's true fighting weight was around 9 stone 4 pounds, although at the beginning of his career he scaled considerably less. He appears to have been a skilful boxer and was described

34. The Belgrave Tavern (North) Finchley, (c.1890), home to two fistic celebrities. (Reproduced by kind permission of Barnet Local Studies and Archives.)

by *The Sportsman* as "showing some very fair science" when losing the final of an 8st 6lb competition on 12 October 1889.

Lee's involvement with boxing did not end when he left the roped arena. He acquired an "establishment in St. James's-road, Bermondsey", known as the Bermondsey School of Arms, where he soon built up a reputation for promoting quality shows. Indeed, in October 1894 *The Sportsman* stated "it is a well-known fact that Bill Lee always provides a capital entertainment"; in the same month the *Sporting Mirror* reported that his "comfortable school of arms is gradually receiving its fair share of the followers of the sport". His promotions mainly featured the lighter men and Professor Lee, as he was now styled, occasionally demonstrated his versatility by additionally acting as a second, referee or master of ceremonies. According to *Fighting Days*, Lee reigned at the Bermondsey School of Arms for six years until licensing difficulties forced him to dispose of the premises. He subsequently accepted an offer to become boxing manager at the West End School of Arms, served in a similar capacity at the Adelphi Club, and took over as landlord of the Hop Pole, Hillingdon Street, Camberwell.

The Kelly's directory for the Barnet area first shows Lee (listed as King) at the address of the Belgrave Tavern in its 1909-10 edition. Like Springall, his active role within boxing seems to have ended when he moved to Finchley, although he continued to make himself available to up-and-coming fighters who sought his advice. (The renowned Matt Wells, who benefited from Lee's expertise whilst training at Whetstone for his first title contest, considered him an "authority on the sport from all angles".) Banks remembered Lee as being "a heavy Port Wine drinker" in his later years and, despite his hands being almost closed by arthritis, "he was always cheerful and loved to talk of his boxing days". He died at the Belgrave Tavern on 7 January 1945, aged 74, from heart disease, and the business was carried on by his son, William King Junior. Incidentally, his daughter continued the family's ring connection by marrying a nephew of Joe Goss.

Last Links

Virtually the last bareknuckle exponent to be buried in the area was Alec Roberts, one of a large family noted for its boxing ability. Alec was in fact equally adept with the 'raw'uns' and gloves, and performed with considerable distinction under both codes. In the latter style he won several major competitions, including twice annexing Bob Habbijam's prestigious "10st 8lb Championship Belt". However, it is his exploits with 'nature's weapons' that we are concerned with here and, although these were somewhat limited, his conduct in the fast disappearing prize-ring brought back memories of the sport's better times.

Born on 1 November 1859, Roberts originally saw service in the 9th Infantry, the 64th Line Regiment and the 93rd Sutherland Highlanders before deciding to make boxing his profession. The first of his three bareknuckle appearances took place during November 1884 against the highly rated Pat Condon in a bout kept such a close secret that no more than twenty spectators were present. The battle was a desperate one, and so even was the match that well into the proceedings not the slightest odds were offered on either man. It took Roberts 1 hour 28 minutes of fierce milling to assert his supremacy; at that point Condon's seconds threw up the sponge to acknowledge their charge's defeat.

Alec's next entry into the prize-ring occurred on 18 June 1887, and necessitated a trip to France since the venue was an island in the River Seine. Possibly the early start of 4 am did not suit him for he began slowly and his opponent, Conny Collins, came very close to scoring a second-round knockout success. However, Roberts recovered and his gameness met with its just reward when, after 15 well-contested rounds, Collins failed to respond to the call of 'time'.

The following year Roberts produced perhaps his best win when he outlasted Marylebone's Jem Hayes in a final set-to in the old style. Again the mill commenced in the small hours of the morning, and once more Alec fell behind in the initial stages. In the 20th round, odds of 2-1 were still freely offered on Hayes but thereafter, showing the greater resource and science, Roberts gradually gained the ascendancy. In total, 64 punishing rounds were fought before Hayes, in an almost unconscious state, was finally retired by his seconds. The boxing journalist and referee Robert Patrick Watson, describing the mill in his memoirs penned around the turn of the century, commented that the battle was "a circumstance to be proud of and talked about for years to come". The sporting press of the time were fulsome in their praise for the courage and fairness shown by the combatants, but this held little sway with the authorities. On 16 July 1888 the men were "charged with having taken part in a prize fight at Rainham [Kent] on the 18th May last", and exactly three months later they were bound over to keep the peace.

With the Hayes contest Roberts's career practically ended, and in the autumn he became boxing instructor to the 1st Batallion Grenadier Guards. He also performed the same role for a leading amateur club, Belgrave BC, enjoying marked success in his tutorial capacity for well over a decade. News of his death, on 5 October 1899 from acute pneumonia, was received with immense sorrow by both organizations.

Roberts was interred on the afternoon of 10 October in a public grave in St Pancras Cemetery, Finchley. Attendance was numerous and the *Sporting Life* remarked that "seldom, indeed, has any boxer or boxer's family had such a mark of respect shown". Amongst those present were well-known fighting men of the calibre of Jem Smith (England's last bareknuckle heavyweight champion), Charles 'Toff' Wall, Jem Hayes, Bat Mullins and Jem Laxton, as well as the deceased's older brothers, Dick and George. The list also included Bob Habbijam, Alec's second against Collins and Hayes, and Jack Roberts (of Drury Lane), later English featherweight champion, who walked over from Edgware where he was in training. The Guards were represented by several non-commissioned officers, all resplendent with their service medals. Afterwards Regimental Sergeant-Major Fowles handed the widow a letter of condolence from all the officers and men of the 1st Grenadiers, together with a cheque towards expenses. Their floral tribute was prominent among a mountain of wreaths, including an enormous one from 140 tradesmen and neighbours, which was tied with the colours of Roberts's old regiment, the 93rd Sutherland Highlanders.

There can be no doubt that Alec Roberts, although now scarcely remembered, was one of the most redoubtable pugilists of his era. Indeed, it was the opinion of Captain Lawrence Fitz-Barnard, an exceptional amateur boxer and author of *Fighting Sports*, that he was one of the best of an elite group of men who had the rare ability to fight just as effectively with the gloves as with the knuckles. Fitz-Barnard even went as far as to say that in this capacity Roberts surpassed John L Sullivan's great rival, the renowned Charlie Mitchell.

Two of Alec's brothers, the aforementioned Dick and George, were also buried at Finchley. Dick died on 29 October 1912 at his residence in Green Lanes, Harringay, and his funeral took place six days afterwards at St Marylebone Cemetery. Although his fame was accomplished with the gloves, he met several opponents who featured in the bareknuckle arena including Mitchell, Bill Goode and Pat Condon. His primary achievement was reaching the final of Billy Madden's open competition for the championship of England in December 1882 when weighing only 10 stone 2 pounds. He later acted "in lieu of a chair" for Mitchell during the latter's prize-fight with Sullivan in France. George, a notable boxing 'professor', was laid to rest on 21 March 1931 near the grave of his brother Dick. At the time of his death, aged 77, he was living in Seymour Road, Harringay.

ENVOI

In boxing, no matter how rapid the changes,
there is not and never will be the variety common to pugilism proper.
One is the substance, the other the reality.

Robert Patrick Watson

It can be seen that there was a dearth of prize-ring contests in the general vicinity of Barnet after the third decade of the 19th century.

This can be attributed mainly to increasing vigilance on the part of the newly established metropolitan local authority police forces (created after the 1835 Munipical Reform Act), which forced changes in the way that matches were arranged. As it became more difficult for hordes of the London Fancy to converge on a site by road without attracting unwanted attention, trains (and river steamers) became the preferred form of transportation to places further afield. The area's popularity as a convenient pugilistic venue was therefore brought virtually to an end.

Initially scheduled trains were used by the fight crowds to reach planned destinations, but the impracticality of this was soon realized and chartered trips to secret locations took their place. Although certain railway companies were less amenable than others in providing such services, the arrangement generally worked well until new legislation, preventing the use of trains for milling excursions, was introduced in 1868. By that time, however, the prize-ring was in a terminal state anyway, and the gradual acceptance of the Marquess of Queensberry's new rules for gloved bouts eventually sounded its death knell. According to his grandson, these rules were passed, with some alterations, by "a committee of the Pugilists' [*sic*] Benevolent Association in 1866". The sport of prize-fighting continued to survive, though, to some degree until around the turn of the century, and even today encounters with the 'raw 'uns' still take place. (Indeed, in his recent autobiography, legendary 1970s unlicensed boxer Roy Shaw described winning £3000 in one afternoon fighting bareknuckle against gypsy opponents at Barnet Fair.)

Whilst its critics rejoiced in the demise of the traditional prize-ring, there were many who mourned the passing of an often corrupt, yet essentially noble, activity. It is hoped that these pages have succeeded in providing the reader with some insight into what was undoubtedly a most dramatic and colourful part of British sporting history.

APPENDICES
&
BIBLIOGRAPHY

———————

APPENDIX A

ADDITIONAL TRAINING IN THE BARNET AREA

Name: Stephen Bailey.
Training quarters: 'Little Tim's', Kitts End.
Under guidance of: Peter Crawley.
Date of contest: 8 April 1828.
Opponent: Isaac Dobell.
Result: Dobell the victor in 23 rounds lasting 21 minutes.
Comments: This was the second meeting between the two men following their initial encounter at Whetstone the previous year.

Name: John Davis, the 'Manchester Black'.
Training quarters: Kitts End.
Under guidance of: Tom Spring.
Date of contest: 9 June 1829.
Opponent: Ned Savage.
Result: Savage forfeited by refusing to come to the scratch and Davis was duly declared to be entitled to the stakes.
Comments: Savage feigned an injury in a bid to cheat his backer. This resulted in the committee of the Fair Play Club passing a resolution "excluding him from all benefits and protections of the Club, recommending pugilists not to spar with, nor suffer themselves to be matched with him, and enjoining the public to discountenance him as a pugilist". (The Fair Play Club had been set up the previous year with the respected Tom Spring as its treasurer. Its subscribers pledged themselves to promote honest conduct within the sport and to employ pugilists to keep order at ringside.)

Name: Ben Burn.
Training quarters: Finchley.
Date of contest: 21 January 1834.
Opponent: Tom Oliver.
Result: Oliver the victor in six rounds lasting 24 minutes.
Comments: This was a battle between two "antiquarians" (Jem Burn's uncle and the then commissary of the prize-ring) following

disparaging remarks made by both men regarding each other's fighting abilities. N B. Sources such as *Pugilistica, Fistiana* and even the *Bell's Life in London* chronology for the year record the fight as taking place on 28 January 1834. However, they are obviously in error since it is fully reported as having occurred "on Tuesday" in the *Bell's Life* edition of Sunday 26 January.

Name: Jack Allen.
Training quarters: Five Bells, Finchley.
Date of contest: 16 February 1836.
Opponent: Izzy Lazarus.
Result: Lazarus the victor in 29 rounds lasting 70 minutes.

Name: James Preston.
Training quarters: Five Bells, Finchley.
Under guidance of: Stephen Bailey (with assistance from Jack Tisdale).
Date of contest: 15 March 1837.
Opponent: George Church.
Result: Church the victor in 36 rounds lasting 63 minutes.

Name: Jack Greenstreet.
Training quarters: Barnet.
Under guidance of: Jack Cullen.
Date of contest: 18 November 1840.
Opponent: Bill Jones (of London).
Result: Jones the victor in ten rounds lasting 25 minutes.

Name: Bill Jones (of London).
Training quarters: Old White Lion ('Dirt House'), Finchley.
Under guidance of: Dick Curtis.
Date of contest: 1 or 2 June 1841.
Opponent: Johnny Walker.
Result: Walker the victor in 35 rounds lasting 57 ½ minutes.
Comments: Regarding the correct date, *Bell's Life in London* of Sunday 6 June stated that the contest occurred "Tuesday last [1st]". However, the newspaper had previously informed its readers that it would take place on the 2nd and the *Morning Post*, which unusually for major journals of the time carried a report of the fight, opted for that day.

Name: Bill Jones (of London).
Training quarters: Five Bells, Finchley.
Under guidance of: Jem Brown.
Date of contest: 17 August 1841.
Opponent: Fred Mason (second fight).
Result: Mason the victor in 21 rounds lasting 29 minutes.
Comments: Jem Brown, who prepared Jones for this contest, was often referred to as the 'Go-Cart Man'; a veteran of several ring battles, he was well known in his day as a second and trainer. Three years earlier he had been in the corner of William Phelps in the latter's fatal bout with Owen Swift, and for that involvement was subsequently sentenced to three months' hard labour.

Name: Cornelius Donovan.
Training quarters: Five Bells, Finchley (with Bill Jones, *see above*).
Under guidance of: Jem Brown.
Date of contest: 17 August 1841 (after Jones–Mason).
Opponent: Joe Rowe.
Result: None reached (fight interrupted by 'beaks').
Comments: Rowe being unable to get to the scratch when the contest was due to be resumed on 7 September, Donovan became entitled to the forfeited stakes.

Name: 'Tom the Greek'.
Training quarters: Five Bells, Finchley.
Date of contest: 20 May 1842.
Opponent: Jack Carter (of London).
Result: 'Tom the Greek' the victor in 17 rounds lasting 30 minutes.

Name: 'Tom the Greek'.
Training quarters: Five Bells, Finchley.
Date of contest: 12 July 1842.
Opponent: Bill Jones (of London).
Result: Jones the victor in 76 rounds lasting 120 minutes.

Name: George Sinclair.
Training quarters: Five Bells, Finchley.
Under guidance of: Jack Sheppard.

Date of contest: 18 July 1843.
Opponent: Ned Adams (second fight).
Result: A draw after 40 rounds lasting 203 minutes. (The men fought until incapable of prolonging the contest.)

Name: Tass Parker.
Training quarters: Five Bells, Finchley.
Date of contest: 27 February 1844.
Opponent: William Perry.
Result: Perry the victor in 133 rounds lasting 152 minutes (Parker down without a blow).
Comments: This was a return contest - the original, on 19 December the previous year, having been interrupted by police.

Name: Joe Bostock.
Training quarters: Duke of York, Ganwick Corner, near Barnet.
Date of contest: 7 May 1844.
Opponent: Bill Turner.
Result: Bostock the victor in 29 rounds lasting 35 minutes.

Name: Tom Brooks.
Training quarters: Five Bells, Finchley.
Under guidance of: Jack Cullen.
Date of contest: 25 March 1845.
Opponent: Jemmy Welsh.
Result: Welsh the victor in 16 rounds after 'beaks' interfered and Brooks refused to enter a second ring.

Name: Harry Cooper.
Training quarters: Barnet.
Date of contest: 9 November 1847.
Opponent: Bill Hayes.
Result: Hayes the victor in 45 rounds lasting 65 minutes.

Name: Andrew Marsden.
Training quarters: Five Bells, Finchley.
Under guidance of: Jack Callaghan.
Date of contest: 21 October 1863.
Opponent: Ned (O')Baldwin.

Result: Marsden the victor in three rounds lasting three and a half minutes.

Comments: The contest was Marsden's regular prize-ring début against his fellow novice (O')Baldwin, who was billed for the occasion as 'Tom Cooper's Big'un' since he was backed by the Birmingham publican. Marsden entered the ring in good shape although slightly fleshy. This was not due to a lack of effort in training but "solely to not having taken up his residence at the Five Bells, Finchley, quite early enough" (*Illustrated Sporting News*). According to *Bell's Life in London* "the match was imagined to be one of more than ordinary interest from the circumstance of its being expected to furnish a fresh candidate for the Champion's Belt". (Marsden did fight for the belt in his next bout but was easily beaten by Joe Wormald.)

Name: Harry Lee ('Bailey's Potman').
Training quarters: Barnet.
Under guidance of: — Nelson.
Date of contest: 8 June 1864.
Opponent: Harry Smith.
Result: Lee the victor in 56 rounds lasting 56 minutes.

Name: 'Punch' Callow.
Training quarters: Anchor Inn, Whetstone.
Under guidance of: Denny Harrington.
Date of contest: 21 July 1880.
Opponent: Jem Carney.
Result: A draw after 74 rounds lasting 122 minutes (referee deemed it advisable to stop fight).

APPENDIX B

ADVERTISEMENTS FOR PUGILISTS' CATERING BOOTHS AT BARNET FAIR
& RACES/FINCHLEY STEEPLE CHASES

Bell's Life in London, **Sunday 18 August 1850:**
Ben Caunt's booth will be erected at Barnet races, where he
will attend himself and cater liberally for the accommodation
of his patrons.

Bell's Life in London, **Sunday 30 August 1857:**
ALEC KEENE AT BARNET - Alec Keene wishes to inform his
country friends and the public in general that he has a booth at
Barnet Fair, where the best accommodation may be relied on,
together with a hearty welcome.

Bell's Life in London, **Sunday 4 September 1859:**
J. Welsh of the Griffin, Borough, will be happy to contribute to the
substantial comforts of the inner man at Barnet, during the fair
and races, at London prices ...

Bell's Life in London, **Sunday 30 August 1863:**
BARNET, BARNET, BARNET FAIR - Professor Welsh, the D'Orsay
of the P.R., host of the Griffin, Church-street, Borough, returns his
sincere thanks to his patrons and friends for their liberal support at
Egham Races, notwithstanding the state of the weather, and begs to
announce that his canvas hotel will be pitched in the horse field
during the fair, stored as usual with the best of the best. Hot and
cold joints, poultry &c, with the requisite attendants, champagne,
port, sherry &c. Bottled ale, stout and first-class coolers.

Bell's Life in London, **Sunday 6 September 1863:**
BARNET! BARNET! BARNET FAIR AND RACES - Alec Keene
and George Brown beg to inform their friends that their spacious
booth will be erected at Barnet Fair as usual; good things will be in
abundance, and at a tariff to suit the circumstances of all. Hot
joints and all vegetables in season. Wines and spirits of the first

quality. Bass's pale ale and Guiness's [*sic*] stout. Again will a hearty welcome be given to all by Keene and Brown; the first cuisine at Barnet Fair. An ordinary on Sunday at London prices.

***Bell's Life in London*, Saturday 27 August 1864:**
JEMMY WELSH AND HIS GRAND CANVAS HOTEL AT FAIRS AND RACES. The famed D'Orsay of the Ring wishes to thank J.C. Heenan and his friends in particular, as well as the general public, for their support at Egham Races and elsewhere. Jemmy Welsh will erect his canvas hotel in his usual place at Barnet during the horse fair and races, will provide the best for his friends as heretofore, and respectfully assures a hearty welcome to all ...

***Bell's Life in London*, Saturday 3 September 1864:**
BARNET. - BARNET FAIR AND RACES (SEPT 4, 5, 6 AND 7). - Alec Keene and G. Brown beg to inform their friends and the public that they will have their large canvas hotel pitched on the usual spot at the above fair and races, where everything of the very best can be had. Hot and cold joints from twelve till four; Moet's champagne, Martell's and Hennessy's [*sic*] brandy, Bass's pale ale, Guinness's stout. Cigars of the very best and a hearty welcome to all.

***Bell's Life in London*, Saturday 2 September 1865:**
BARNET CATTLE AND PLEASURE FAIR AND RACES, MONDAY, TUESDAY, AND WEDNESDAY, SEPT 4, 5, AND 6 - Alec Keene and George Brown beg to inform their friends and the public that they will have their booth on the old spot on the road, opposite the Fair Field, near the Red Lion. Hot joints each day, and poultry, with all vegetables in season. Cold collations. Wines and spirits of the best brand. Cigars and the fragrant weed of the very best. An ordinary this day at one for half past precisely. Everything at London prices.

***Bell's Life in London*, Saturday 2 September 1865:**
BARNET FAIR AND RACES - Jesse Hatton, of the King's Head, Bear-street, Leicester-square will attend the above amusements on Monday, Sept 4 and two following days with his commodious water proof canvas hotel, wherein every accommodation and delicacy of the season may be obtained, including hot joints, pastry &c. Jesse

will be stocked with the finest Burton and other ales, and the best London stout, porter, and spirits. The choicest wines may also be had, consisting of Moet's champagne, and port, sherry, with others of the oldest vintage. Every charge will be most moderate and Jesse can assure those who favour him with a visit that nothing shall be wanting on his part to make that pleasant, and his usual civility will be strictly adhered to.

Bell's Life in London, **Saturday 2 September 1865:**
BARNET FAIR AND RACES. - The renowned Jemmy Welsh will be at the above races on Monday, Tuesday, and Wednesday next, at the original spot, namely the horse fair, where his friends and visitors generally will meet with the best of cheer. Pork, geese, and ducks, both hot and cold, with every variety of vegetables in season.

Bell's Life in London, **Saturday 2 September 1865:**
G. CROCKETT AND G. SIMM'S GRAND BOOTH AT BARNET FAIR. - These great caterers for sportsmen and the public will erect the famed Blue Anchor booth, first on the right from London in the cattle field. Poultry, hot and cold joints, all vegetables in season, all spirits, wines, malt and hops, draught or in bottle, A 1. Open on the 3d, continue during Monday, Tuesday and Wednesday. Remember Crockett and Simm's booth.

Bell's Life in London, **Saturday 25 August 1866:**
... Alec Keene and G. Brown will have their canvas hotel at Barnet Cattle Pleasure Fair and Races on their old spot on the main road, opposite the fair field. Sept 3 and following days when they hope for a continuance of the patronage they have hitherto received. Due notice will be given in our next.

Bell's Life in London, **Saturday 1 September 1866:**
...Alec Keene and G. Brown's canvas hotel at Barnet Pleasure Fair and Races on the old spot. Hot joints and poultry every day, with all vegetables in season. Cold collation. Moet's champagne, wines and spirits of the best brands. Bass's pale and Edinburgh ales on draught at London prices. Hot dinners provided for large or small parties by giving two hours' notice. Everything A 1...

Bell's Life in London, **Saturday 1 September 1866:**
BARNET - BARNET FAIR AND RACES - Bob Travers (Champion of the Light Weights) will have his spacious booth erected at Barnet Fair, for the supply of first-class refreshments. Hot joints, with vegetables in season, always ready. Choice wines and spirits, Bass's ale, Guinness's stout, Hennessy's [*sic*] Martell's brandies, Moet's champagne of the best brands, draught ale and stout of the best quality. On this occasion he will be assisted by Job Cobley, Patsy Reardon and J. Drew ...

Bell's Life in London, **Saturday 1 September 1866:**
BARNET FAIR AND RACES. - JESSE HATTON. - The famed caterer for the public of the King's Head, Bear-street, Leicester-square, will have No.3 booth, which will be the A 1 caravansarai at the races and cattle fair. All hot joints, vegetables, ducks, fowls, the savoury porcine delicious bird of Michaelmas, partridges, grouse &c, Moet's champagne, wines and spirits, supernaculem [*sic*] ale, foaming takard [*sic*], and fragrant weed. A hearty welcome, comfort and accommodation. Tariff within reach of all. No.3 booth.

Bell's Life in London, **Saturday 1 September 1866:**
JACK HICKS AND GEORGE CROCKETT AT BARNET FAIR AND RACES - The booth of these famed caterers will be on the horse fair and race ground, where the best of all things will be served - hot joints, vegetables, the Michaelmas bird, luscious with sage and onions, poultry, game &c, champagne, wines, spirits, bottled ales, cigars, foaming tankard, and fragrant weed. The best of accommodation, and at prices to meet all with hearty welcome.

Sporting Life, **Saturday 1 September 1866:**
BARNET FAIR AND RACES - Bob Travers, Champion of the Light-weights, will have his spacious booth erected at Barnet Fair, for the supply of first-class refreshments. Hot joints, with vegetables in season; wines and spirits of the first quality, Bass's ale, Guinness's stout, Martell and Henessey's brandy, Moet's champagne of the first brands, and a hearty welcome to all.

***Sporting Life*, Wednesday 28 August 1867:**
... A. Keene and G. Brown will have their Canvas Hotel at Barnet Fair and Races, where they will be happy to see their friends.

***Bell's Life in London*, Saturday 31 August 1867:**
Alec Keene and G. Brown ... N.B. They will likewise have their monster canvas hotel at Barnet Fair and Races, Wednesday, Thursday, and Friday, Sept 4, 5, 6 in their old place opposite the fair field, where they will provide each day hot dinners, with dairy-fed pork, and the savoury Michaelmas bird. All vegetables in season in galore. A. Keene and G. Brown will be happy to give all their friends a hearty welcome ...

***Bell's Life in London*, Saturday 31 August 1867:**
BARNET FAIR. - Jesse Hatton will have his canvas hotel on his old spot at the large fair, which will be No.3 booth, where he will have dinners, roast and boiled, of all in season. Charrington's ales, Reid's stout, Moet's champagne, Martell's brandies. A 1. Dinners 2s 6d each, joints fish &c, included. Everything warranted the best. Do not forget the French cook arrived from Paris.

***Bell's Life in London*, Saturday 29 August 1868:**
BARNET RACES, CATTLE AND PLEASURE FAIR - Alec Keene and George Brown beg to inform their friends they will be on their old spot opposite the horse fair at the above gathering; likewise they will have their monster booth in the horned cattle field and will also cater in the Stand on the race day. Hot dinners each day, including poultry, joints of all descriptions, with all vegetables in season; wines and spirits of the best brands, Bass's ale and Guiness's [sic] stout; cigars of the finest quality ...

***Bell's Life in London*, Saturday 5 September 1868:**
BARNET RACES, CATTLE AND PLEASURE FAIR. - Alec Keene and George Brown the far-famed caterers, are now at Barnet where they have made great preparations for Monday, having the Grand Stand (being race day), when their friends may rely on finding everything A 1 as usual. Hot dinners, poultry included, provided, with all vegetables in season ...

Bell's Life in London, **Saturday 19 December 1868:**
FINCHLEY GRAND CHRISTMAS STEEPLE CHASES, BOXING
DAY, DEC 26 AND MONDAY DEC 28. - ALEC KEENE AND
GEO BROWN - These far-famed caterers inform their friends and
the public in general that they will cater at the Grand Stand at the
above races, where, as usual, everything will be provided A1 in
their well-known style. Hot joints, soups &c, ready half an hour
before each race. N.B. K. and B. will attend on the course this
day, Dec 19, at two o'clock p.m, to let part of the ground.

Sporting Life, **Wednesday 23 December 1868:**
FINCHLEY GRAND CHRISTMAS STEEPLE CHASES, BOXING
DAY, DECEMBER 26, AND MONDAY, DECEMBER 28. - ALEC
KEENE AND GEORGE BROWN - These renowned purveyors
will have the catering of the Grand Stand at this popular
meeting, where they have made immense preparations for the
accommodation of the public. All of the best will be provided.
Hot soups and hot dinners will be ready half an hour before
each race. The viands, edibles, &c., will be of the best, and meet
the tariff of all.

Sporting Life, **Wednesday 23 December 1868:**
BOXING! BOXING!! BOXING!!! - FINCHLEY STEEPLE
CHASES - JEMMY WELSH, THE GREAT CATERER - The
D'Orsay of the P.R. has secured No.2 booth. To give his bill of fare
is superfluous - the usual 'fog-defying' soups, hot joints, and all
that gladdeneth the heart of man, especially the sportsman. Mr.
Welsh, in anticipation of the meeting on Saturday and Monday
next, has made all preparations. Mr. Robinson and other
celebrated bookmakers can be found at Welsh's. Call and give
Jemmy a turn, and learn the whole of the winners.

Bell's Life in London, **Saturday 26 December 1868:**
JEMMY WELSH AT FINCHLEY STEEPLE CHASES - By special
desire, this great caterer will be at the Finchley Steeple Chases, at
No.2 Booth next the Grand Stand, this day (Saturday), Boxing
Day, and Monday, the 28th. The best of Christmas fare will be
served, and to reiterate the good things supplied by the D'Orsay
of the Ring would be a hundredth-told tale. Mr. Welsh will make it

a real Boxing Day at Finchley. Mr. Robinson and other celebrated bookmakers will make Welsh's their rendezvous on Saturday (this day) and Monday next.

Bell's Life in London, **Saturday 4 September 1869:**
JEMMY WELSH, THE ACKNOWLEDGED GREAT CATERER. - Barnet Fair and Races, this day (Saturday), Sept 4 and Monday and Tuesday next, Sept 6 and 7. The grand booth for all hot and cold joints. The savoury bird of Michaelmas, sage of the escular [*sic*] in abundance. The whole resources of Jemmy Welsh's new tavern, Marquis of Granby, Granby-place, New-cut (a few doors from the Artichoke) will be brought in requisition. The D'Orsay of the Ring, the renowned second of Tom Sayers, gives good welcome to all friends at his new drum in the Lower Marsh, Lambeth and has a still warmer greeting at Barnet Fair and Races. Remember the booth on the right from London. All will know the old spot.

Bell's Life in London, **Saturday 3 September 1870:**
BARNET FAIR AND RACES. - JEMMY WELSH, THE GREAT CATERER. - Barnet Fair, for cattle, horses, sheep &c and the races will be held Sept 5, 6, and 8, in the usual place, Prickler's Hill, on the right hand of Barnet Town. The D'Orsay of the Ring will have his canvas hotel in the midst of the fair, and serve the very best; the finest view of the races on Wednesday, Sept 7 at Jemmy Welsh's booth. Special and extra accommodation will be provided for friends and the public, by Jemmy Welsh, at the well supported cuisine. Let old friends and new support the A 1 booth at Barnet Fair.

APPENDIX C

COGNOMENS OF FEATURED CHARACTERS

American Giant: Charles Freeman

Bailey's Potman: Harry Lee
Bath Butcher: Sam Martin
Bath Carpenter: Tom Gaynor
Battersea Gardener: Tom Oliver
Bendigo: William Thompson
Benicia Boy: John C Heenan
Big Ben: Ben Bryan (Brain)
Birmingham Youth: Phil Sampson
Black Diamond: Tom Cribb
      -        Jem Ward
Bloomsbury Pet: Tom Maley
Brighton Bill: William Phelps
Buckhorse: John Smith
Bungaree: John Gorrick

Chelsea Snob: Alec Reid
Chelsea Star: Jem Hood
Child of Promise: James Preston
Cicero of the Ring: Harry Holt
Cock of Walham Green: Joe Bevan
Colonel: Tom Reidie

Deaf 'un: James Burke
Death: Stephen Oliver
Disher: Tom Juchau
D'Orsay of the Ring: Jemmy Welsh
Dutch Sam: Samuel Elias

East End Sailor Boy: Tom Smith
Elastic Potboy: Job Cobley

Game Chicken: Henry Pearce
Gasman: Tom Hickman
 (also known as Gas-light Man)
Go-Cart Man: Jem Brown
Great Gun of Windsor: Tom Cannon
Gybletts' Chicken: Bill Fitzmaurice
 (also known as East-end Chicken)

Hammersmith Cowboy: Jack Wil(l)sden
Hammersmith Jack: John Read
Hellgate: Lord Richard Barrymore
Herefordshire Pippin: — Evans

Jack of Finchley: John Brunston
Jaw Breaker: Joe Tibbett
John Bull Fighter: Josh Hudson

King of the Tinkers: Arthur M'Ginnis

Little Barnet Poulterer: — Perkinson
Little Fighting Butcher: Bill Purdue
Little Wonder: Owen Swift
Lively Kid: Ned Stockman
Liverpool Slasher: George Sinclair
Long Tom: Thomas Marshal

My Nevvy: Jem Burn

Nonpareil: Jack Randall

Paddington Pet: Ned Thompson
Pet of the Fancy: Dick Curtis
Pocket Hercules: Anthony Noon

Ratcliffe Highway Rough: George Church
Redditch Needle-pointer: Tom Paddock
Royal Professor: Ned Donnelly
Ruffian (old): John Symonds

Sage of the East: Tom Owen
Sailor Boy: Harry Jones
Slashing Painter: Tom Brooks
Sprig of Myrtle: Ned Brown
Stalybridge Infant: Sam Hurst
Star of the East: Barney Aaron
Streatham Youth: Ned Neale

Terrible Tom-Boy: Richard Foster
Terrible Welchman: James Francis
Tinman: Bill Hooper
Tipton Slasher: William Perry
Tom the Greek: Thomas Murray

Uncle Ben: Ben Burn

Westminster Pet: Byng Stocks
Whiteheaded Bob: Ned Baldwin
Wychwood Forester: Bill Turner

Young Broome: William Evans
Young Dutch Sam: Samuel Evans
                 Aaron Moss
Young Gas: Jonathan Bissel
Young Molineaux: James Wharton
  (also known as Jemmy the Black/Moroccan Prince)
Young Ruffian: Jack Firby
Young Rumpsteak: Peter Crawley
Young Spring: Harry Woods

APPENDIX D

G<small>LOSSARY</small>

Back slums	Low insalubrious neighbourhood
Bait	Food, especially for horses
Beak	Justice of the Peace, magistrate
Bottom	Courage and fortitude – "[He] died all game and bottom" (Lord Byron)
Bruiser	Prize-fighter – "Let no one sneer at the bruisers of England – what were the gladiators of Rome, or the bull-fighters of Spain, in its palmiest days, compared to England's bruisers?" (George Borrow)
Bye-Battle	Minor contest
Chairman	One whose occupation it was to carry passengers in a sedan chair
Claret	Blood – "I tapped his claret; I broke his head, and made the blood run" (*The 1811 Dictionary of the Vulgar Tongue*)
Coal-whipper	One who unloads coal from the hold of a ship
Cordwainer	Shoemaker
Corinthian	Man about town, particularly a wealthy amateur of sport
Cove	Fellow
Cross (X)	Fixed or 'thrown' contest; that which is not fair and square
Cross-buttock	A throw to the ground over and across the buttocks – "... the most fatal of all falls, and has, on many occasions, decided the issue of a battle..." (*Fistiana*)
Fancy	Enthusiasts of a particular amusement or pursuit, especially followers of the prize-ring
Fogle	Silk handkerchief

Higgler	"one who sells provisions by retail" (Samuel Johnson)
Hocussing	Stupefying with drugs, particularly for a criminal purpose
Jarvey	Hackney-coachman
Keg-meg purveyor	Butcher selling inferior meat
Mawley	Hand – "Tip us your mawley; shake hands with me" (*The 1811 Dictionary of the Vulgar Tongue*)
Mill	Pugilistic encounter between two persons
Muff	Someone awkward or stupid at an athletic pursuit
Ordinary	Set meal at a fixed price
Pedestrian	One who practises feats of endurance walking
Peruke	Wig
Postboy	Boy or man who rides posthorses, postilion
Prigged	Stolen
Rookery	Cluster of mean, densely populated tenements inhabited by the lowest classes
Sharper	"A tricking fellow..." (Samuel Johnson)
Snip	Tailor
Snob	Shoemaker or cobbler
Toddler	One who travels on foot
Trap	Constable, one whose business is catching offenders; also a small carriage
Trotter	Foot
Turn-up	"... Properly a casual and hasty set-to" (*Tom Cribb's Memorial to Congress*)
Weed	Tobacco
Whip	One skilled in the art of coachmanship

BIBLIOGRAPHY

The following is a list of sources which provided useful material during the compilation of this book. Those containing facts directly appertaining to prize-fighters or prize-fighting in the Barnet area are marked with an asterisk; the remainder were consulted for general background information.

BOOKS

*Amateur of Eminence, An, *The Complete Art of Boxing* (1788)
*Angle, B J, *My Sporting Memories* (1925)

Barnett, R D (ed), *Bevis Marks Records Part IV The Circumcision Register of Isaac and Abraham De Paiba 1715-1775* (1991)
Batchelor, Denzil (ed), *The Boxing Companion* (1964)
*Bee, Jon, *Boxiana; or, Sketches of Modern Pugilism*, vol IV (1824)
*Belcher, Thomas, *The Art of Boxing* (1820)
*Bettinson, A F and Outram, W Tristram (ed), *The National Sporting Club Past and Present* (1901)
*Brady, James, *Strange Encounters* (1947)
*Brailsford, Dennis, *Bareknuckles: A Social History of Prizefighting* (1988)
*Brailsford, Dennis, *Sport, Time & Society* (1991)
Briggs, Martin S, *Middlesex Old and New* (1934)
Brown, Walter Edwin, *The St. Pancras Book of Dates* (1904)

Chesney, Kellow, *The Victorian Underworld* (1970)
*Cleveland, Harry E, *Fisticuffs and Personalities of the Prize Ring* (1924)
Cohen, Louis, *Reminiscences of Johannesburg and London* (1924)
Conan Doyle, A, *Tales of the Ring and the Camp* (1922)
*Cunningham, Allan, *The Lives of the Most Eminent British Painters, Sculptors and Architects*, vol II (1829-33)

Davies, J Alford, *Barnet and its Personalities, or its Associations with Literature & Life* (1913)
*Donnelly, Ned, *Self-Defence or The Art of Boxing* (1879)
*Dowling, Francis, *Fistiana; or The Oracle of the Ring* (1866)
*Dowling, Vincent, *Fistiana; or The Oracle of the Ring* (1841)
*Drackett, Philip Arthur, *Fighting Days Incidents in the Life of Bill Lee* (1944)

*Egan, Pierce, *Anecdotes of the Turf, the Chase, the Ring and the Stage* (1827)
*Egan, Pierce, *Boxiana; or, Sketches of Ancient and Modern Pugilism*, vol I (1812)
*Egan, Pierce, *Boxiana; or, Sketches of Modern Pugilism*, vol III (1821)
  Emden, Paul H, *Jews of Britain A Series of Biographies* (1943)
  Erskine, (trans), *The Memoirs and Adventures of the Marquis de Bretagne, and Duc D'Harcourt, etc*, vol II (1743)

  Fewtrell, Thomas, *Boxing Reviewed; or, The Science of Manual Defence, etc* (1790)
  Fitz-Barnard, Capt Lawrence, *Fighting Sports* (1921)
*Fleischer, Nat, *Black Dynamite*, vol I (1938)
*Ford, John, *Prizefighting The Age of Regency Boximania* (1971)

  Godfrey, Capt John, *A Treatise upon the Useful Science of Defence* (1747)
  Green, Benny, *Shaw's Champions G.B.S. & Prizefighting from Cashel Byron to Gene Tunney* (1978)

  Harper, Charles G, *The Great North Road* (1901)
  Hartley, R A, *History & Bibliography of Boxing Books* (1989)
*Hartley, R A, *Jack Scroggins 19th Century Pugilist* incorporating 'The Memoirs of John Scroggins' and 'Annals of Pugilism' by Richard Humphreys (1989)
*Henning, Fred, *Fights for the Championship The Men and Their Times*, 2 vols (1902)

  Joliffe, Graham and Jones, Arthur, *Hertfordshire Inns and Public Houses* (1995)

*_Kelly's Barnet, Finchley, Hendon, Southgate & District Directory For 1894-5_
  Kelly's Barnet, Finchley, Hendon, Southgate & District Directory For 1898-9
*_Kelly's Directory of Barnet, Finchley, Hendon, Golders Green, Southgate and District For 1909-10_

*Lynch, Bohun, *Knuckles and Gloves* (1922)

*Mace, Jem, *Fifty Years a Fighter* (A 1989 reprint from the original 1908 edition)
*Magriel, Paul (ed), *The Memoirs of the Life of Daniel Mendoza* (1951)
  Matthews, Bill, *The English Boxing Champions (1872-1910) and Record Book* (1990)
  Meller, Hugh, *London Cemeteries An Illustrated Guide and Gazetteer* (3rd edn, 1994)
  Mendoza, Daniel, *The Modern Art of Boxing* (1790)
*Miles, Henry Downes, *Pugilistica: The History of British Boxing*, 3 vols (1880)
  Mitchell, R J and Leys, M D R, *A History of London Life* (1958)

Mitchell, Sally (ed), *Victorian Britain, an Encyclopaedia* (1988)

*Oxberry, William, *Pancratia, or a History of Pugilism* (1812)

Pigot and Co.'s London & Provincial New Commercial Directory, For 1823-4
*Platt, Charles, *Famous Fights and Fighters* (1920)
*Pugnus, *History of the Prize Ring*, Parts I & II (1876-1877)

Queensberry, The Tenth Marquess of, *The Sporting Queensberrys* (1942)
Quennell, Peter (ed), *Byron A Self-Portrait Letters and Diaries 1798 to 1824*, vol II (1950)

Reading, The Marquess of, *Rufus Isaacs, First Marquess of Reading 1860-1914* (1942)
Reid, J C, *Bucks and Bruisers Pierce Egan and Regency England* (1971)
Rutherford Davis, K, *Deserted Medieval Villages of Hertfordshire* (1982)

*Sawyer, Tom, *Noble Art* (1989)
*Shaw, Roy, *Pretty Boy* (1999)
Stevens, Horace William Pettit, *Old Barnet* (1886)
*Swift, Owen, *The Hand-book to Boxing* (1840)

Trevelyan, G M, *Illustrated English Social History*, vols 3 & 4 (Pelican Books edn, 1964)

Walford, Edward, *Village London, the Story of Greater London*, vol I (1983)
Watson, Robert P, *Memoirs of Robert Patrick Watson: A Journalist's Experience of Mixed Society* (1899)
Weinreb, Ben and Hibbert, Christopher (ed), *The London Encyclopaedia* (1983)
Wheatley, Henry B, *Hogarth's London* (1909)
Wheatley, Henry B, *London Past and Present*, vol II (1891)
Widdicombe, S H, *A chat about Barnet and its History* (1912)

MANUSCRIPTS

*C O Banks Collection, Barnet Local Studies and Archives

*Census Returns 1841 HO107/438 Registrar's District Barnet, f13
Census Returns 1881 RG11/654 Registrar's District Battersea, f37
Census Returns 1891 RG12/440 Registrar's District Clapham, f171

*Elisa Anne Salvin Diaries, Barnet Local Studies and Archives (MS 6787)

*Gaol Book for the Liberty of St Albans and Borough of St Albans Quarter Sessions, 1786-1807, Hertfordshire Record Office (ref LSGB 2)
  Gaol Book for the Liberty of St Albans Quarter Sessions, 1819-1828, Hertfordshire Record Office (ref LSGB 4)

*Liberty of St Albans Quarter Sessions Minute Book, 1786-1793, Hertfordshire Record Office (ref LSMB 2)
*Liberty of St Albans Quarter Sessions Roll, 1784-1791, Hertfordshire Record Office (ref LSR 1)
*Liberty of St Albans Quarter Sessions Roll, 1793-1799, Hertfordshire Record Office (ref LSR 2)
  Liberty of St Albans Quarter Sessions Roll, 1819, Hertfordshire Record Office (ref LSR Bdl 6)
  Liberty of St. Albans Quarter Sessions Roll, 1820, Hertfordshire Record Office (ref LSR Bdl 7)

NEWSPAPERS AND MAGAZINES

**Annals of Sporting and Fancy Gazette*

*Barnet Gazette
**Barnet Press, Finchley News, &c*
*Bath Journal
**Bell's Life in London and Sporting Chronicle*
  Bell's Life in Sydney
**Bell's Weekly Messenger*
**British Luminary, or Weekly Intelligencer*

  Chicago Tribune
**County Chronicle and Weekly Advertiser, for Essex, Herts., etc.*
**Courier, The*

  Daily Advertiser
  Daily Courant
**Daily Universal Register*
**Diary; or, Woodfall's Register*
**Dundee Courier and Argus*

**Famous Fights in the Prize Ring*

Famous Fights Past and Present (Police Budget Edition)

Gale's Licensed Victuallers' Mirror
Gazetteer and New Daily Advertiser
General Evening Post
  Gentleman's Magazine, and Historical Chronicle
  Glasgow Herald
Globe and Traveller

Illustrated Sporting and Theatrical News and Record of General and Domestic Intelligence
Illustrated Sporting News and Theatrical and Music Review

Kent's Weekly Dispatch and Sporting Mercury

Licensed Victuallers' Gazette and Hotel Courier
Lloyds Evening Post and British Chronicle
London Chronicle
London Evening-Post

Middlesex Journal, and Evening Advertiser
Mirror of Life
Morning Chronicle, and London Advertiser
Morning Herald
Morning Post and Daily Advertiser
Morning Post and Gazetteer

  New York Herald
  New York Times

Oracle Bell's New World
Oracle, and the Daily Advertiser

Pall Mall Gazette
  Penny London Post, or, The Morning Advertiser
Pierce Egan's Life in London, and Sporting Guide
Pierce Egan's Weekly Courier
Public Advertiser
Public Ledger, and Daily Advertiser

St. James's Chronicle; or British Evening-Post
  St. James's Gazette
  Saunders's News-Letter and Daily Advertiser

Sporting Chronicle
*Sporting Life
*Sporting Magazine, etc
*Sporting Mirror
Sporting Mirror and Dramatic and Music Hall Record
*Sportsman, The
*Star, The
*Sun, The

*Times, The
True Protestant Mercury

*Weekly Dispatch
Welwyn Times
*Whitehall Evening-Post
*World, Fashionable Advertiser

INDEX
(Figures in italics refer to illustrations)

UP TO SCRATCH